FINANCIAL LITERACY FOR TEENS MADE EASY

A BEGINNER'S GUIDE

to Budgeting, Saving, and Investing—Build Real-World Money Skills and Take Control of Your Financial Future with Confidence

LUCAS STERLING

TOP TIER PRESS

CONTENTS

INTRODUCTION

Money. It probably feels like just another thing adults talk about, a boring topic that's part of the "real world" you're supposed to worry about someday after you graduate, get your first "real" job, or move into your own place. Maybe you've tuned out when your parents complain about bills or your teachers drone on about budgeting. But here's the truth: money is already part of your life. Every time you decide whether to buy lunch with friends, download a new game, save up for sneakers, or accept payment for babysitting or mowing lawns, you're making choices about money. And those choices, no matter how small they seem, matter more than you might think.

Let's be real. Money isn't just green paper, numbers in an app, or the stuff grown-ups argue about. It's way bigger than that. Money means freedom. Money unlocks options and helps you do the things you actually care about. Want to buy concert tickets? Save up for your first car? Travel, help friends, or even invest in something cool that grows your wealth over time? All of that starts with understanding money, not someday, but right now.

Learning how money works puts you in the driver's seat instead of just riding along while someone else makes the choices.

If you feel like you don't know much about personal finance, you're not alone. Most schools barely teach it. Many parents don't talk openly about their own financial mistakes or successes. A lot of what you see online about making money is either too complicated or sounds fake (because, hint: a lot of it is). You might even feel frustrated, confused, or just plain bored whenever the topic comes up. If so, good news: this book was written for you. No boring lectures. No intimidating jargon. Just practical advice you can actually use, starting today, whether you've got $10 from your last birthday or a paycheck from your weekend job.

You might be wondering, why should I care about money now? Isn't this the kind of stuff for adults? Here's the secret nobody tells you: the sooner you start learning this, the easier your life will be later. Imagine knowing exactly what to do with your first paycheck, never stressing about surprise expenses, being able to choose the college you want because you saved up, or even having the freedom to say yes (or no) to opportunities because you're not worried about money. That's not just grown-up stuff; that's confidence, independence, and power. And you can start building it now.

Here's the deal: money affects every part of your daily life. It shows up in your relationships, your goals, your opportunities, and even your mental health. Ever felt left out when friends go out because you couldn't afford it? Ever stressed about buying something you really wanted versus saving up for something bigger? Those feelings are real, and they're tied to how you handle your money. The good news is that managing money well isn't about being rich or obsessing over every penny. It's about knowing what matters to you, setting goals, and making your dollars match your dreams.

This book isn't about turning you into a Wall Street genius overnight or expecting you to live off ramen noodles forever. It's about helping you become the boss of your own financial life, starting with the basics and leveling up as you grow. We'll walk through earning (even if you're still in school), saving smarter, spending without guilt, building real credit, and yes, even investing, which is far less scary than it sounds. You'll learn how to avoid common traps that trip up adults, dodge debt drama before it starts, and use your tech-savvy skills to stay ahead. Social media gives you more ways to make money, spend it, and even lose it, so let's make sure you know how to win at your own game.

One of the biggest myths about money is that you have to be born rich or get lucky to succeed. But the truth is, most financially confident people didn't win the lottery or inherit millions. They simply started learning early, made smart moves, and kept going even when things got tough or mistakes happened. It doesn't matter if your family talks about investments at the dinner table or avoids the subject. What matters now is that you have the power to take control of your money story, starting from wherever you are.

And if you're thinking, "But I'm just a teenager, I barely earn anything!" don't sell yourself short. Whether you're making cash from dog-walking, selling stuff online, working part-time, or getting an allowance, these are your first chances to practice skills that will set you up for life. The habits you build now, like tracking where your money goes, choosing what's worth spending on, building up savings, or even growing a little extra through investing, make a massive difference down the line. Think about this: would you rather scramble to figure things out when you're deep in student loans, or already have confidence and a plan for any curveball life throws at you?

Throughout this book, you'll find step-by-step guides, real-life stories (the good, the bad, and the awkward), and tips that cut through the nonsense. There's no one-size-fits-all approach here. You'll create a money plan that fits your life, your goals, and your style. Worried you have to give up all fun to succeed? Relax. Smart money management isn't about saying "no" to everything. It's about saying "yes" to the stuff that really matters and knowing how to make those choices confidently.

A lot of adults wish they'd learned about money sooner. They look back and think, "If only someone had told me how to handle a paycheck, use a credit card, or avoid getting into debt." Guess what? You don't have to wait until you've made expensive mistakes. You can skip some of the hardest lessons by learning the basics now. That means more choices, less stress, and way more control over your future.

If you're reading this, you're already taking a major step ahead of the crowd. You're curious. You want to level up. And that curiosity, the willingness to learn a few simple strategies, will pay off in ways you can't even imagine yet. Whether you dream of traveling the world, paying for college, starting your own business, helping family, or simply not worrying about money, it all starts here.

So, why care about money even if adulthood feels far away? Because money is the ticket to your freedom, your independence, and your choices. The sooner you understand how it works, the sooner you can use it to shape the life you actually want, not the one you settle for. This book isn't just another class assignment. It's your guide to becoming the kind of person who's confident, prepared, and ready for whatever comes next, long before anyone expects you to be.

Ready to take control? Let's dive in, break down the mysteries, and turn money into your superpower. The journey starts now.

UNLOCK YOUR MONEY ADVENTURE JOURNAL

Ready to make learning about money fun, empowering, and practical?

As a thank-you for reading this book, I've created something special just for you: **The Money Adventure Journal.** This no-fluff guide is packed with fun challenges, smart trackers, and reflection pages that help you earn, save, and spend like a money pro. It's your space to dream big, plan smart, and build confidence with every dollar you make.

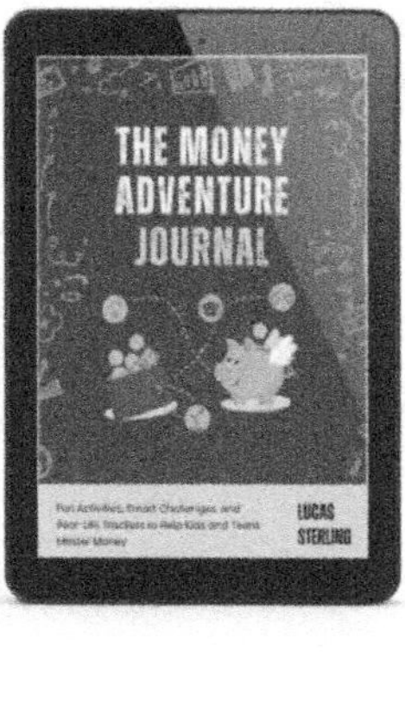

Inside your journal, you'll find:

- Cool activities and real-life money missions
- Trackers to help you save, spend, and share wisely
- Fun pages for setting goals and celebrating wins
- Simple tips to grow your money skills and confidence

👉 **Access Your Companion Workbook**

Visit: **https://content.toptierpress.com/free-money-adventure-journal**

Or scan the QR code below to get instant access!

CHAPTER 1

WHAT IS MONEY, REALLY?

Have you ever stopped to think about what money really is? Why do we use coins and bills instead of just swapping things directly with each other? How did money become something everyone trusts, whether it's in the form of cash, cards, or even apps on your phone? You might wonder why some forms of money feel safer or easier to use than others, or how all these different kinds actually fit into daily life. If you've ever saved up for something special, paid for a snack, or debated whether to swipe your card or pay with cash, you're already part of the big story of money, and there's a lot more to it than just spending. This chapter will help you understand where money started, why it works the way it does, and what it means for you as you start managing your cash and choices.

The Origins of Money and Its Role as a Tool

Think about when you wanted something your friend had, like a rare trading card, your favorite snack, or a concert ticket. Maybe you tried trading your own stuff to get it like offering two packs of chips for one extra concert wristband. This can be awkward if the trades aren't equal or you both want different things. If you don't want what the other person has, or if you and your friend value things differently, trades stall. This is where the earliest problems with bartering showed up, even for people long before us.

Societies needed a way to trade that worked for everyone, no matter what they wanted in return or who they were dealing with. Over time, people started using items that almost everyone agreed were useful, desirable, or hard to get. These became early forms of money. In some places, shells or shiny stones were popular. Other groups preferred chunks of metal. Pretty soon, these items became the "go-between" whenever anyone wanted to swap things, like food, clothes, or services. Instead of asking, "Do you want my apples for your shoes?" people could just use these special objects to pay. That made trading much easier.

Let's clear up a word you'll see a lot: "currency." This just means anything a group accepts as money, something trusted enough to be used in buying and selling almost anything. You might think of currency as coins, bills, or even numbers moving on your banking app, those are just forms it takes. What matters is that currency makes it possible to trade with anyone, even strangers, and get what you want or need.

People kept experimenting with what to use as money. Metal coins became favorites because they last, don't break easily, and can be carried in a pocket. Governments began making coins with official symbols on them so everyone knew they were real. This saved time, since nobody had to weigh chunks of metal or argue about what they were worth. Eventually, paper money showed up. It was lighter, easy to carry, and could have government promises or official messages printed on it. Later, as technology raced ahead, money was no longer just something you held in your hand. Now, you can pay with a card, tap your phone, or even buy things online using digital money. You can move money around without ever touching cash.

Why did all these changes happen? In one word: trust. People trust money works. They believe they can spend it today or save it for when they really need it. You can think of money like a charge-up bar in a video game. Each dollar or coin is a bit of energy you save up, ready for whenever you want to do something like buy art supplies for a school project or enjoy a day with friends. Money stores value, which means you can use it later for something else, not just right now.

There's another big piece: money is a tool, not just a thing to spend the second you get it. Ever saved up for a new phone or game? Or should it be spent carefully so that you can donate to a cause you care about? Each choice shows money turning ideas into reality. You pick what matters to you, and money acts like the key that unlocks options. This control means your decisions and your dreams don't have to wait until you're older or have a job. Whether it's getting supplies for a class project, going out for pizza with friends, or saving for a trip, money provides you the power to act on your goals.

Being able to trade is only part of the story. Money lets you save for future plans and smooth out life's ups and downs. Maybe your family sets money aside for emergencies or uses it to pay bills when someone is out of work. You might keep birthday cash safe until a big sale comes around. These habits help people do things over time, not just in the moment. Saving and planning aren't always as exciting as big spending, but they help you set yourself up for freedom, making sure your future self thanks you.

Money also matters for sharing and helping others. With it, you can donate to charity, support a team, or chip in for a group gift.

When people pool money, they can help make bigger things happen than one person ever could alone.

As you get more familiar with money, you start to see both its strengths and limits. You can save up for a dream, like a big trip abroad, but you still need to decide how to handle lunches, bus fares, or emergencies along the way. Choices about spending, saving, and giving show money's real power, and some of its limits, too. These questions shape how you use money, and that's where understanding it starts to pay off in real life.

Money's Impact: Capabilities and Daily Influence

Why does money matter so much to people, and how do you fit it into your world as a teen? You already know money is a tool, but how much can this tool actually do for you? Picture yourself with extra cash from a birthday or a first job. Maybe you dream of snagging the newest headphones, saving for a car, or just having money to grab boba after school with friends. Most people use money to get things they want or need, and it goes far beyond just shopping sprees.

When you buy a burger, pay for an app, or split the tab at a pizza shop, you're using money as a way to trade for goods and services. This function is called a "medium of exchange." Whether you hand over cash, swipe a card, or scan your phone, you're using something other people agree has value to make life simpler. Back in the day, people had to trade physical stuff to get what they needed. Imagine swapping three graphic novels for a haircut, it wouldn't be easy or convenient. Money removes all that hassle so you don't need to barter.

Money also helps you manage your things for the future. Let's say you work a summer job and stash away part of your pay. When you save like this, you're using money as a "store of value." This means you can keep your money now and use it later when something you really want or need comes along. Picture saving for a concert in a few months or skipping extra snacks so you can buy gaming gear later. If you hid your money under your mattress, it would still buy you things weeks or months from now. Some teens set small goals, like saving for sneakers or tickets, while others want to see their savings grow for long-term dreams.

Now and then, you have to make choices about how to use what you have. You check whether those jeans you want are actually worth twice the price of another brand. You might write down a list before going out, or use a budgeting app to track what you plan to spend at the mall or online. In these moments, money acts as a "unit of account." It gives you a way to compare the costs of different things, set budgets, and keep track of your goals. One friend says, "I only have enough for either the movie or the new controller." You start thinking, Which one matters more to me this week? Decisions about earning, spending, and saving all start with this simple way to measure value.

Money lets people make plans, protect themselves from emergencies, and enjoy fun experiences. With some savings put aside, you don't have to panic if your phone falls and cracks or you need a quick ride home. Money can make you feel independent and give you choices, do you want to work extra hours for that festival, or keep your weekends free? Do you treat friends to smoothies or chip in on a group gift? These choices add up and start to shape how you handle your freedom.

But here's the catch: as much as money can buy stuff, it can't solve every problem. It won't fix a fight with friends, erase anxiety about grades, or create real confidence in yourself. Imagine someone who consistently pays for lunch, believing it will earn them friends. Occasionally it works for the day, but real friendships go way beyond what you buy. For example, if you buy a cool jacket similar to what everyone else has, you might hope it will help you fit in. You might feel left out after all or realize there's always something new you're missing. Money cannot satisfy your inner desires.

Companies are adept at manipulating your emotions. Ads make it seem like you "need" things to be fulfilled, or that buying the latest drop will end your FOMO. Before clicking "add to cart," ask yourself a few things:

- Is this a true need (shoes for gym) or just a want (limited edition kicks)?
- Will this make my life easier right now, or will I forget about it in a week?
- Am I buying because I really like it—or because everyone else is?

Making these kinds of choices helps you take control instead of going along with every trend. Sticking to your own goals lets you spend and save for what really matters.

Every day, you use money in more ways than you realize—handing over cash, texting friends to pay you back, using apps for group gifts, or tapping a card on the bus. People now have all sorts of ways to pay and keep track of their money, and understanding these modern forms is part of knowing how money fits into daily life.

Types of Money: Cash, Cards, Apps, and Crypto

When you reach into your pocket and find a crumpled bill or a pile of coins, you're holding the most straightforward kind of money: cash. It's easy to understand because you can see and touch it. You might use cash to buy a snack from the vending machine, pay for a slice of pizza at a food cart, or hand a friend a few dollars for gas money. Cash is handy in person and makes small, face-to-face deals quick. Even so, walking around with a pocket full of bills isn't always practical. If you lose your wallet, that money is just gone, with almost no chance of getting it back. Plus, cash is useless for online shopping, which limits what you can do when everything from game credits to sneakers needs to be bought online. Some places don't even accept cash anymore, so you might find yourself stuck if you're not carrying a card.

People your age are probably more used to seeing shiny plastic cards get swiped at checkout than huge stacks of cash. Debit cards work like digital wallets that are tied to your bank account. When you use a debit card for coffee, video games, or a new hoodie, your money moves straight out of your account. The process is simple: you can swipe it, tap it (if it's contactless), or stick it in a chip reader. You can even pull cash from an ATM using your debit card when you really need it. Debit cards help you keep track of spending, because you can check your account online or through an app and see exactly where the money went. But there's a caution: if you spend more than you have, your card might get declined, or you could be hit with overdraft fees. It's also possible to lose your entire balance if someone gets access to your card and spends your money.

Credit cards look almost the same as debit cards, but they work differently. When you use a credit card, like borrowing your parent's card to shop online or using your own beginner card, the money isn't coming straight out of your account. It's like using someone else's cash for a while, with a promise to pay it back. This is handy if you find a killer sale but don't get paid until next week, or if you have an emergency and need some wiggle room. Some credit cards offer rewards, cashback, or special discounts, which can feel like free money. The catch? Anything you borrow must get paid back, usually with interest if you don't pay it off quickly. Missing payments can lead to debt, fees, and a negative credit history that follows you for years. Swiping, tapping, and inserting chips also work with credit cards, so using one at a store feels pretty much the same as using a debit card.

Cards make life easier when you aren't carrying wads of cash, but they have their risks. You might not always see your money leaving your account, so it's easy to overspend or forget about a small payment until your balance is lower than expected. If your card information is stolen, hackers can spend your money or run up debts before you even notice, though banks can sometimes help you get a refund.

With all sorts of digital payment apps buzzing around, you can move money without even reaching for your wallet. Venmo, PayPal, and Apple Pay connect to your bank account, card, or even a digital wallet. Maybe you pay your friends for concert tickets using Venmo, chip in for a group pizza through PayPal, or skip pulling out your card by tapping your phone with Apple Pay at the grocery store. These apps are super fast and perfect for splitting bills; no more awkward math with cash or waiting for someone to find exact change. Most apps show you a record of every payment, which helps you see where your money is going and reminds you who owes whom after a night out. Still, digital apps can be a mess if you send money to the wrong person, forget your password, or pick a weak one that lets someone else drain your funds. They work great when you're online but can leave you stuck if your phone battery dies or you're in an area with no internet access.

Cryptocurrencies like Bitcoin have popped up everywhere. Maybe a friend at school is convinced crypto will make them rich, or you've seen stories about NFTs on TikTok. Instead of bills, coins, or balances on a bank app, crypto exists entirely online in special encrypted networks. People use digital "wallet" apps to send or receive it. Using crypto is a bit like trading digital collectibles: there's no bank involved, and anyone in the world can participate.

Some stores even accept Bitcoin, and there are crypto ATMs in certain cities. However, crypto can feel more like a risky guessing game because its price constantly changes. A single coin could be worth hundreds one day and much less the next. While crypto payments can be fast, losing your private key or sending money to the wrong address can mean those funds are gone for good.

For most teens, crypto is something to understand and stay aware of, rather than something to use for everyday spending.

Each form of money plays a part depending on what you need: cash works for face-to-face swaps, cards for shopping and holding money safely, digital apps for paying friends or buying online, and crypto as a curiosity or risky investment tool. Knowing your options helps pick the right one for each situation, and avoid stress when something goes wrong.

Now that you understand where money comes from, how it works, and the many forms it can take, you're better equipped to make smart choices with your own cash. Whether you're saving for something special, deciding how to spend your birthday money, or just figuring out when to use cash versus a card or app, knowing money's real purpose helps you stay in control. As you practice using money wisely, you'll build habits that protect your future, give you freedom, and help you reach your goals without falling for every flashy trend. Money isn't magic, but used right, it's a powerful tool that can open up opportunities and let you bring your ideas to life.

CHAPTER 2
HOW TO ACTUALLY MAKE MONEY (YES, EVEN AS A TEEN!)

I still remember the first time I held actual cash from a job I had done myself. It wasn't thousands or even hundreds; it was just enough to buy a few things I wanted and to feel something new: pride. Back then, I had no idea how to find work that fit my busy school schedule or where to start with all the paperwork and rules. It felt like stepping into a completely different world, one where money didn't magically appear but came from effort, planning, and a bit of courage.

What if you could skip some of that confusion? What if making money wasn't something you had to wait for, but something you could start doing right now, on your own terms? That's exactly what many teens are discovering today, and it's more achievable than you might think.

Finding Jobs and Gigs That Work for You

If you want to start making money as a teen, you don't have to wait until adulthood to get moving. Plenty of teens earn cash, learn cool skills, and gain confidence in jobs that fit school and life. This starts with understanding the options out there. Some jobs have scheduled shifts and clear hours. At a grocery store, you clock in as a cashier, work your four-hour shift, and clock out. In other gigs, you control when you work: walking dogs for neighbors, designing digital artwork, or helping a local business post on social media. Think about what fits with school and your other activities. Want weekends off for sports? Flexible gigs work best. Prefer a steady routine? Try a set-schedule job. Always check the age rules near you since some jobs have age minimums, limits on hours, or require paperwork. Parents often need to sign off if you're under sixteen.

Classic and Creative Ways to Earn as a Teen

Popular picks with a long track record:

- Babysitting younger kids for family friends
- Lawn mowing, raking leaves, or shoveling snow
- Bagging groceries or stocking shelves at a supermarket
- Working as a lifeguard at community pools (with certification)
- Tutoring classmates in your strong subjects

Newer options that feel more like side hustles:

- Creating and selling digital art, stickers, or jewelry on platforms like Etsy (with parent help if required)
- Walking dogs or pet-sitting through neighborhood apps
- Selling gently used clothes and shoes on Depop or eBay
- Helping older adults set up their phones or computers
- Running social media pages for a local shop or band

Some teens land their first gig by asking around, offering yardwork services door-to-door, or checking at a family-run diner. Others chase a passion, like a teen soccer player running after-school drills for younger kids and getting paid for it. A friend who plays guitar can offer music lessons. Another who loves photography can shoot photos for friends' social media pages or special events. Real-life stories show how teens take what they like and turn it into eager clients and some extra cash.

Finding Work That Fits You

Start by asking yourself a few questions. Do you want to work by yourself or in a group? Are you okay speaking with adults you don't know, or do you prefer sticking with people in your social circles? How much time do you have after classes, sports, or family stuff? Even twenty minutes a few days a week can add up. Grab a notebook or use your phone:

- List your skills. Can you draw, play piano, organize, fix things, or explain homework easily?
- Write what excites you. Do you love gaming, teaching, cooking, or being outdoors?

Match this list with job ideas nearby. If you like animals, dog walking or pet sitting works well. If you thrive talking to people, jobs with customers at shops or food spots might fit. If you're introverted, selling crafts online or tutoring one-on-one feels more comfortable. Remember, what worked for one teen may not fit another. For example, Devon had a passion for skateboarding. He started teaching younger kids on weekends and saved up for a new board. Or Priya, who started baking birthday cupcakes for neighbors and friends, slowly building a steady stream of small orders.

Making the First Move: Search, Apply, and Start

Finding jobs or gigs is easier if you break it down. Start by looking close to home. Check the community center, ask at your school office, or peek at family and friends' workplaces. Many parents hear about local jobs before teens do. Next, check online. Job boards and neighborhood apps (like Nextdoor) post help-wanted notes for pet care, leaf raking, or basic errands. For remote freelance work (design, writing, editing), some platforms allow teens with parent permission. Never share personal info unless you're sure the source is safe, and check with an adult first.

Applying is not as scary as it sounds. Your first resume can highlight class projects, volunteer events, or leadership in clubs. For example:

- Participating in a food drive at school? That shows reliability.
- Organized a group for a science fair? That counts as project management.
- Babysitting your siblings? Real responsibility.

When reaching out, short and friendly messages work best. In-person: "Hi, I heard you might be looking for someone to help. I'm interested and reliable." Online, introduce yourself with similar honesty. After applying, it's okay to check in a few days later: "Hi, I wanted to follow up and see if you've reviewed my application. I'm still interested." If you don't get the first job, don't sweat it. Every message you send, every little gig you attempt, builds up your skills and gets you closer to your first paycheck.

Every step teaches you something new, not just about making money, but about who you are and what you can do. As you try new types of side jobs or work, you'll see new strengths, and friends and family will notice. Whether it's pocket money or your first real payday, every win matters. Getting started opens the door to bigger ideas, more options, and new ways to handle what you earn.

Creative Money-Making Ideas and Managing Your Earnings

Whether you land a side hustle or your first job, what matters is what comes after that. Teens across your school or community are getting creative about ways to bring in extra cash, and you don't need a driver's license or an adult-like resume to play the game. Think about Alex, a sophomore who realized last year that barely used sneakers and trendy shirt drops gather dust in his closet. He started flipping them on Depop, and within a couple months, he'd cleared out old gear and had real money landing in Venmo for the first time. Then there's Maya, who picked up her first gig babysitting her neighbor's twins on Friday nights. She likes knowing exactly how much she'll make in a week, and the parents trust her enough that when they get home, there's always a little extra for pizza or streaming.

Not everyone feels like digging through their closet or sitting for kids, though. If you're more into tech and less into yardwork, you could start a small gig doing digital artwork commissions on Etsy. Want a quick hit of cash? Your phone is already your greatest ally in this situation. Download an app that connects you to local dog owners who will pay for you to walk or pet-sit. Jamal, an outgoing junior, mixes it up; he mows lawns, then records funny TikToks about his weirdest yardwork fails, and gets Venmo payments straight from regular clients, plus the occasional $5 Cash App tip from a TikTok follower. If you're solid at math or have skills in a subject like Spanish, offering tutoring to younger students can pay per session, and you decide your schedule. The point is, whether your vibe is creative, hands-on, low-key, or social, there's a way for you to earn.

Spreading out income from a bunch of these sources? It's easy for money to disappear fast if you don't have a plan. The first step to feeling that money is truly "yours" is tracking it; every dollar, every time. Skip the paper mess and open your notes app or set up a super-basic spreadsheet in Google Sheets. Make a section for each stream: cash jobs, app payments, or actual paychecks. After you finish a babysitting gig, type the date and amount into your log. Made $30 from a hoodie sale? Pop that number in too, maybe with a photo or quick note about what sold fastest. Got your first paycheck from the smoothie shop? Snap a picture, add the after-tax total, and you won't forget how much dominos into your bank account.

Here's how it looks step-by-step:

1. Open a notes app or spreadsheet.

2. Title three sections: "Cash Jobs," "Online Sales," "Paychecks."

3. Add a row whenever you get paid:

- "March 4 - Babysitting - $40"
- "March 8 - Sold vintage shirt - $27"
- "March 12 - Juice World - $82 (after taxes)"

4. Check your totals at the end of each week and see where most of your money comes from.

You might want to level up and use a money-tracking app (like Mint or EveryDollar) just for teens. These can link to your bank, or you can input your cash flow manually. Being consistent with money tracking isn't about being boring; it's about feeling excited when you notice that the earnings from small jobs are adding up and you're halfway to purchasing those headphones or sneakers you desire.

Beyond tracking, keeping your money organized matters more than you'd think. You don't want cash floating loose in your backpack or digital dollars stuck in six apps. Physical cash fits well in labeled envelopes tucked in a safe spot - think "Fun," "Savings," and "Big Goals." That said, teens with access to digital banks like Step or current can store, split, and move money between virtual "jars" for better control. Setting up automatic transfers to saving buckets (as soon as money hits) helps keep treats from draining your whole balance. If friends pay you through different apps, make it a habit once a week to move everything you can into a main account. Losing track of $3 or $5 here and there adds up, so keeping everything in one or two places keeps you in control.

Watch out for the classic mistake of accidentally spending every dollar the day it arrives. Try pausing before buying in-app loot boxes or ordering another boba. Even putting away $5 out of every $20 you earn builds money confidence. Small wins early on mean you'll have options when you want to buy concert tickets, sign up for a new activity, or cover an "emergency" pizza night. Developing strong habits now can prevent awkward and financially difficult moments in the future.

Once money starts coming in, new questions pop up. Teens who organize earnings get ahead not just with dollars but also with handling taxes, schedules, and future paperwork. Earning is just a start; what you do next, like figuring out paystubs or setting goals, takes money skills to the next level. All these moves stack up to give you freedom, and that's what makes early earning worth it.

What to Know Before You Start Working and Building a Strong Money Mindset

Getting your first paycheck or earning cash on your own feels pretty great. It's exciting to see your hard work pay off, whether you pick up a part-time job, offer tutoring, start babysitting, help neighbors with chores, or launch a creative gig online. With so many new earning opportunities, it's simple to focus on the "how much" aspect. There's another piece you can't skip: being ready before you even start working. Feeling confident about money is easier when you know how to fit a job into your life, understand how you'll get paid, and have a healthy attitude about it all.

Time Management for Earning Teens

Balancing school, family, activities, and your first money-making gig can get overwhelming fast. A soccer practice that runs late, a math test coming up, or your sibling's birthday; now imagine adding a shift at your new job to the mix. Without a plan, you might forget commitments, double-book yourself, or end up exhausted.

Here are steps to keep your week organized and stress levels down:

- Write down everything that's already on your calendar —classes, homework, sports, family duties, and social events.
- Use a planner app or a simple notebook to map out your week, blocking out time for each activity.
- Before saying "yes" to a shift or new job, check your schedule and think about how it will affect your other responsibilities.

- If you start feeling stretched, talk to your boss, coach, or family about what's on your plate.
- Remember that school needs to be a top priority. If grades slip or you're missing sleep, it's time to adjust.

Smart time management isn't just about checking boxes. It's about giving yourself a balanced life, so earning money feels rewarding, not draining.

What to Know About Taxes When You're a Teen Worker

Seeing your first paycheck can bring a shock. "Wait, where did part of my money go?" Here's the deal: If you work for a company, you'll probably fill out a "W-4" form before you start. This form tells your employer how much money to take out of each paycheck for taxes. Taxes help pay for things like roads, schools, and safety services.

What shows up on your pay stub as "deductions" is money subtracted for:

- Federal income tax
- State income tax (in most states)
- Social Security
- Medicare

If you make $100, and $10 comes out for taxes, your "take-home pay" is $90. This is what gets deposited or handed to you. If you make more than a certain amount in a year, you may need to file a tax return. That means filling out forms (usually online) in the spring to show how much you earned and paid in taxes. Occasionally, you get money back.

If you work for cash, let's say you're babysitting, mowing lawns, or selling art, taxes won't get taken out right away. You may still need to track your earnings and report them when tax season comes. Always save a little, just in case taxes are due later. Understanding this stuff isn't about being an expert. It just means fewer surprises and better planning.

Top Tips for First-Time Teen Workers

Starting out at your first job or gig can be a mix of excitement and nerves. To help, here's a list of useful tips for feeling in control:

- Always show up on time. If you're late or need to miss, let your boss or contact know as soon as possible.
- Maintain a small notebook or a digital note to monitor your assignments and deadlines, ensuring nothing is overlooked.
- Ask questions if you're unsure about something.
- Check your work and follow through with any promises you make.
- Listen carefully to feedback, and don't be afraid to make mistakes; mistakes are how you learn.

If things go wrong, like miscounting change or forgetting a small task, own up to it. Apologize, fix it if you can, and use it as a learning chance. Standing up for yourself is part of the job too. If you feel uncomfortable, confused, or treated unfairly, talk to a trusted adult or your supervisor.

Building a Respectful and Healthy Money Mindset

A healthy money mindset starts before your first payday. Money takes effort to earn, and respecting your time (and your paycheck) builds long-term habits.

Imagine getting $50 from your new gig. You feel like celebrating, and it's gone before the week's up: new headphones, snacks, a quick splurge. Next time, try splitting your earnings into "save," "spend," and "give" jars. Put some aside for goals, use a bit for fun, and if you want, help out with something bigger than yourself.

If you slip into habits like spending every dollar or not keeping track, pause and ask, "Is this helping the future me?" Treating money with care means you enjoy what you have, avoid regret, and set up possibilities for later, like a driver's license, a trip, or something you want. Making money doesn't just give you stuff; it helps you feel proud, responsible, and ready for more.

Now that you've got the tools to find jobs and gigs that fit your life, understand how to start working, and build a smart money mindset, you're ready to take charge of your financial future. Whether it's your first babysitting job, selling art online, or mowing lawns, each step teaches you more about your strengths and what matters to you. By managing your time well, tracking every dollar, and thinking ahead about spending and saving, you're setting yourself up for real success, not just today, but for everything ahead. So go ahead, explore opportunities, ask questions, and remember: earning money is just the beginning of the adventure toward independence and confidence in handling your own cash.

CHAPTER 3

BUDGETING BASIC

TELLING YOUR MONEY WHAT TO DO

"I swear, my money just disappears the second I get it." That's a sentence many of us know all too well. Whether it's from a weekend job, birthday cash, or just an allowance, the excitement of having money can quickly fade when you realize it vanished faster than you expected. But what if you could actually tell your money where to go instead of wondering where it went? Imagine having a simple way to make sure you have enough for what really matters, whether that's saving for something big or still enjoying those little treats on the side. It's not about giving up fun; it's about deciding what counts first and taking control so you're prepared for anything life throws your way. This chapter is all about helping you find control and confidence with your cash.

Why Budgeting Matters and How to Prioritize Needs vs. Wants

Picture this: you've just been paid for working weekend shifts at the smoothie shop, or maybe your parents added a little extra to your account for helping around the house. Suddenly, ideas flood in. You could grab concert tickets with friends, start saving for that sleek new phone, or finally try that all-you-can-eat sushi spot everyone keeps posting about. Yet somehow, the cash always seems to vanish faster than free pizza in the school cafeteria. That's where budgeting changes everything. It turns money stress into something you can manage and even enjoy.

Budgeting isn't about saying "no" to fun. It's more like creating your playlist before a big road trip. You choose what tracks, or in this case goals, play first so you're not stuck with silence when you want your favorite song later. When you make a budget, you tell your money exactly where to go instead of wondering where it went. That's real control. It means you can save for the things that truly matter, like a digital drawing tablet, while still having enough for Starbucks Thursdays or the latest game. And that feeling when a big expense is coming up, like prom tickets or a birthday gift, and you already have cash ready? That's real freedom, and it's all in your hands.

Most people run into problems with money not because they don't earn enough, but because they don't have a plan. Without a budget, it's simple to overspend on things that flash across your feed or to give in when friends invite you out three times in a single week. If you know what you want to buy, you won't worry when you swipe your card at the vending machine or Target. Budgeting places you in control. Every dollar gets a job, whether it's helping you snag that next-level gaming headset or covering late-night rides home after study group. The magic comes from deciding ahead of time, not reacting after your balance dips below $5.

Before you set up any numbers or lists, there's a trick that makes budgeting work: knowing the difference between needs and wants. Needs aren't always dramatic, but they seriously affect your life if you ignore them. Food, basic clothes, a way to get to school, and school supplies are needs. No one likes showing up hungry or without headphones for e-learning, but you can't function without the basics. Even the data plan for your phone might make the need list if you're commuting, working, or staying in touch with family.

Wants are things you enjoy but can live without or put off if needed. Eating pizza on Fridays, buying the newest sneakers that are trending on TikTok, or upgrading to Spotify Premium are all desires. If they disappeared for a month, life might feel a little less fun, but it wouldn't fall apart. Sometimes, it gets blurry. Maybe you need new shoes because your old ones have holes. That's a need. Are you interested in a second, flashy pair because it matches the color of your favorite streamer's gear? That lands in the want zone.

Getting real about what counts as a need or a want doesn't mean you have to be strict or miss out on fun. It means you get to enjoy your wants with less guilt because you've looked after your needs first. Start by tracking what you spend for a week. Identify the expenses that are essential for survival, such as lunch, bus pass, and school project supplies, and those that are considered extras, like bubble tea runs, extra game credits, and a designer water bottle. This simple step gives you more control than most adults have over their paychecks.

With your spending in full view, it's easier to make smart money choices. If you know you are saving for a summer trip with friends, you might choose to postpone that impulse purchase from TikTok or restrict "treat yourself" spending to once a week. Setting aside a bit of "fun money" each month makes it possible to enjoy your wants without wrecking your goals. Look for student discounts, team up with friends for group deals, and compare prices online before buying. Deciding ahead that you'll pick one treat or upgrade each month helps avoid impulse buys and peer pressure splurges. Soon, you'll notice your leftover cash grows and your stress shrinks.

Sorting your needs and wants and deciding where your money will go creates a clear path forward. Once you know what's essential and what's extra, making an actual budget and mapping out your monthly money plan, gets much easier. With this foundation, you'll be able to put together a plan that actually works for real life and gives you more freedom, not less.

Building Your First Budget and Crafting a Personalized Monthly Plan

After sorting needs from wants and figuring out why budgeting matters, you're ready for action. The next part is making your own budget, putting everything you've learned into play. This isn't about limiting yourself or cutting out all the fun; it's about making moves with your money that match what's important to you. Every dollar you get, no matter where it comes from, is a chance to choose.

Start by getting clear about where your money actually comes from. It can be regular, like a paycheck from a part-time job or a weekly allowance, or less regular - money you get for babysitting, holiday gifts, or helping a neighbor. Add all the amounts together for the month. Here's what it might look like:

- Part-time job: $200/month
- Allowance: $20/week ($80/month)
- Babysitting: Average $20/week ($80/month)
- Birthday money or gifts: $40/month (averaged out)

When you add those up, your estimated monthly income is $400. It helps to grab a notebook, open your notes app, or use a budget worksheet and write down each type of income and its expected amount. Being realistic is key. Guess low if you're not sure.

Now, start listing every expense you can think of for the month. This part takes honesty. Go through a week or two in your head or check your transaction history. There are two types of expenses. Fixed: these don't change much and come up on a regular schedule. Examples:

- Phone bill: $30
- Monthly bus pass: $45
- Automatic transfer to savings: $20

Variable expenses are where most of your choices are. Some examples:

- School lunches/snacks: $30
- Clothes/gear: $25
- Streaming (music, shows): $10
- Weekend spending: $40
- Boba Fridays: $20
- Venmo'd a friend for pizza: $8
- App or game purchases: $12

Don't skip the little or occasional buys—they add up. Even if you use cash or pay family back, those count as expenses. Add it all together. Maybe your total expenses this month are $240.

Now comes the formula: take your total income ($400), subtract your expenses ($240), and get what's left. In this case, you'd have $160 as your "freedom." That's money you can use for whatever feels right: keeping it in savings, going out with friends, or setting it aside for something big.

What if your expenses are higher than what you bring in? This is when your needs-versus-wants work helps most. Go back through your list, marking every item as a need or a want. Maybe you realize you spent $20 on digital add-ons for a game you quit playing, or your snacks bill doubled this month. This isn't about guilt, it's your chance to shift dollars to things that matter more. If cutting isn't enough, you can look for ways to earn a little extra, like another babysitting job, selling old clothes, or checking if your family could increase your allowance for extra chores.

Walk yourself through this every month:

1. Write down all sources of expected income, even if some are estimates.
2. List every expense you can think of, looking at regular bills first, then everyday and occasional spending.
3. Subtract expenses from income for your dollar amount of "freedom."
4. If you're in the negative, make changes—either by trimming wants or adding new income sources.
5. Give every dollar a job, whether it's for spending, saving, or big-picture goals.

Let's say you have $40 left after the basics. That could fund a concert ticket, a side trip with friends, or boost a savings goal for new headphones. The cool part is, you're the one choosing what to prioritize.

Budgets are subject to change. They grow with you. Some months you want to spend more on social stuff; others you'd rather save. Things happen. Maybe you get a gift or lose a gig. Update your numbers and keep moving forward. Try out tools or apps designed for budgeting if you're into tech. Even keeping notes in your phone and checking in once a week can help you spot when you're meeting your goals or drifting off track.

By sticking with this, you start to notice where your money goes without stressing over every cent. Every round of budgeting gives you more freedom and confidence to steer your course.

Choosing Your Budgeting Tools and Staying Financially Secure

Everyone's money plan needs action to work. Tracking where money actually goes is what makes a budget more than just numbers on paper. Without knowing how much you're spending and on what, that budget you set up turns invisible and can't protect you against big surprises. It's like plotting a route on your phone's map, but never checking if you're going in the right direction. Turning a plan into real control starts with picking a tool to help you see and steer your cash decisions each day.

Three Strong Ways to Track Your Budget

Digital Apps

Many teens reach for their phone first, so using a budgeting app comes naturally. Apps like Mint, YNAB (You Need a Budget), EveryDollar, and Goodbudget help you track every dollar as it moves in and out. Most of them link to bank accounts, show you pie charts, and notify you when you're getting close to a limit. Some are free, while others offer better extra features for a fee. A student who works weekends and gets paid through Venmo could connect their checking account to an app like Mint, watch paychecks show up, and see exactly how much was spent on coffee, sneakers, or movie nights. It updates on its own, so there are no missing details. Apps are awesome for people glued to their screens who want quick check-ins anywhere.

- **Pros:** Fast, automatic updates, useful graphs, reminder notifications, easy to use on the go
- **Cons:** Needs Wi-Fi or data, logging in can take time, sometimes hard to customize or fix errors

Traditional Notebooks or Bullet Journals

Some people connect better with old-school tracking. Writing out what you spent in a paper notebook or a bullet journal mixes budgeting with creativity and reflection. You buy a pack of gum or lunch, jot it down in your log, and, over time, each page tells a story. One artist saves receipts in a pouch and tapes them next to pencil sketches of their lunch, mixing art and spending records. You don't need apps or passwords, just a pen and a notebook you like. Each week, add up totals in each budget category and compare with your plan.

- **Pros:** Customizable, chance for creative touches, doesn't need Wi-Fi, helps with mindfulness
- **Cons:** Can feel slow, easy to skip entries, no reminders unless you set alarms

Spreadsheets (like Google Sheets or Excel)

For people who like flexibility or want more control, spreadsheets give you a personal dashboard. Free templates online make starting simple, or you can set up basic categories and formulas yourself. Someone with a babysitting side hustle might track gigs and expenses, color-code categories, and make new tabs for each month. Google Sheets works on a phone and computer, so you never lose access. Data entry is manual, but you see everything at once.

- **Pros:** Highly flexible, easy sharing for group money (like club treasuries), can add graphs and notes
- **Cons:** Takes time to learn, manual entry, not as automatic as apps

Finding the Right Method for You

Picking a style has more to do with who you are than what's "best." The perfect system doesn't exist. What matters is what you'll actually stick with. If your phone is part of your daily life, using an app keeps things quick and convenient. Visual thinkers might prefer a bullet journal filled with doodles, stickers, or color-coded categories. Spreadsheet fans often like seeing all their numbers together and may add personal notes or reminders in a comments column.

You can always switch methods or even combine them. For example, one person might track daily spending in a notebook and then enter the totals into a spreadsheet once a week. Try one method for a month. If it feels annoying, boring, or hard to keep up, that's completely normal. Change it until tracking feels natural. Consistency, not perfection, is what makes the difference.

How Tracking Beats Financial Shortfalls

Staying in touch with your actual spending helps keep you out of trouble. One teen checks her bank app every few days and logs her card purchases when she gets home. By seeing her balance drop faster than expected, she notices when her fast-food habit eats into weekend plans and cuts back in time to avoid overdrafting. Even if you don't have much income, regular check-ins help you spot when you're close to your limit so you can say no or wait before buying. Patterns begin to appear, such as spending a little each day on snacks that add up by the end of the month. You start using your money for things that matter instead of letting it slip away without realizing it.

Making Healthy Habits Stick

Life gets busy, and even the best budget can get pushed aside. To keep on track:

- Set reminders or alarms, like a Sunday night alert to review last week's spending
- Tie tracking habits to things you already do (update your app on bus rides, log expenses after work shifts)
- Make it fun with rewards for a full week of tracking, like an extra treat or new playlist
- Forgive yourself for missing a day or two; just pick back up

With enough practice, keeping tabs on your money feels less like a chore and more like freedom. Soon, you'll spot problems before they mess up your plans and feel stronger every time you hit your goals, even small ones. Staying on top of your budget can turn worries into confidence and boredom into motivation.

You're now ready to take real control of your money after understanding why budgeting matters, how to build a plan that fits your life, and the tools that can help you stay on track. Budgeting isn't about missing out; it's about choosing what matters most and feeling confident in those choices. As you practice tracking your income and expenses, you'll start spotting patterns, making smarter decisions, and turning your goals into reality. The more you work with your budget, the easier it becomes to handle surprises, save for cool stuff, and enjoy the freedom that comes from knowing exactly where your money goes. This chapter sets the stage for a future where you call the shots, and that's a pretty awesome place to be.

CHAPTER 4
SAVING WITHOUT FEELING BROKE

Have you ever felt excited to get some money, only to watch it disappear too quickly on snacks, clothes, or hanging out with friends? Maybe saving sounds like saying no to fun or missing out on cool things. But what if saving money could actually help you have more choices and feel more in control instead of less? How can you save without feeling broke or like you're giving up what you want right now?

This chapter dives into the real truth about saving. It's not about being strict or missing out; it's about making your money work for you so you can handle surprises, reach your goals, and still enjoy the things that matter most. You'll discover simple ways to build a safety net, set realistic goals, and create habits that make saving easy even when your income or plans change from week to week. By the end, you'll see that saving gives you freedom, not limits, and that small steps can grow into big wins over time.

Why Choosing to Save Sets You Up for Success

Getting your money for the first time changes how you see the world. Suddenly, you don't have to ask for everything. But as soon as cash lands in your wallet, it's almost like it starts calling your name. Fast food on the way home, a new hoodie that appears online, streaming subscriptions, or a spontaneous movie outing with friends, all are enjoyable, yet it is remarkable how effortless it is for your money to quickly disappear. Most teens feel that pull to spend as soon as they get paid or get their allowance. Saving it? Sometimes that sounds boring or even unfair, like you have to say no to stuff just to see a number grow in your account.

Here's what people don't talk about enough: saving isn't about missing out. It's about getting more out of what you already have and building your life exactly the way you want. When you spend all your money, you enjoy immediate fun but restrict your future options. Compare two scenarios: one teen gets $40 from babysitting, spends $18 on delivery and a movie, then grabs a $15 graphic tee. It's all gone. When friends ask if you want to hit a show next weekend, you're stuck. The other teen spends $10, puts $30 away, and a week later, has $60 after another job. Now concert tickets or new sneakers aren't out of reach. Saving means your options get bigger every time you make a choice, not smaller.

The best part is, saving doesn't have to mean locking away giant chunks of money. It's more like putting a little bit to the side each time you get paid. If you save $5 from every $30 paycheck, in ten weeks you'll have $50, enough for a last-minute trip, a fancy dinner, or a birthday present for a close friend. It's not an amount that changes your life in one go, but it gives you the kind of control that spending can't touch. Even five bucks a week can make a real difference. Think about what pops up during a regular month: someone's birthday, an old pair of headphones breaking, a school event, food runs after practice. With some savings, you're not forced to skip out or scramble to explain why you're always broke right before the fun starts.

There's another side to all of this. The stress most teens feel around money rarely comes from not having enough for cool stuff. It often comes from that sick feeling when your wallet is empty and something comes up. You can't replace a phone screen that shatters in your backpack. You have no backup plan if you leave your skateboard at the park and someone grabs it. Or maybe your friends want to go on a random weekend trip, but you can't ask your parents for more money after spending everything on snacks and impulse buys. Suddenly, you've got to say no, not because you hate fun, but because you spent it all already. That's when not saving stops just being annoying and starts being a hassle.

When you build up even a small buffer, those what-if moments go from being mini disasters to just a part of life. Say you set aside $2 every time you get cash, even if you only get paid twice a month. By the end of the school year, you'll have over $30 tucked away, without really feeling the loss. That $30 almost always comes in handy; maybe your earbud breaks during finals week, or you want to chip in for pizza when your group hangs out at the park. You're not scrambling. You're not stressed. Even your parents notice you aren't asking for a rescue all the time, and fights about money start to cool off.

Saving empowers you to take charge, rather than experiencing money as a fleeting entity. You're the one deciding when, how, and what you spend on, not the other way around. Sure, it's easy to worry that by saving you'll miss out, but saving is actually what lets you say yes more often. You get to choose your fun and not let money decide for you. That's freedom.

Getting good at this isn't about turning into a savings robot, and it's not just about stacking up cash for the super cool stuff. It's about knowing you're covered for the sudden stuff that always seems to pop up, a cracked screen, lost gear, or plans popping up out of nowhere. With a little saved, you're always ready for what comes next, not just what you can see coming.

Building Your Safety Net and Setting Savings Goals

Feeling in control of your money isn't just about saying no to a new hoodie or not grabbing takeout with friends. When you start making money choices for yourself, you realize freedom and chill are way better than stressing about running out of cash. One huge move that grows your sense of control is having a plan for life's curveballs and for your own dreams. That's where emergency funds and goal-setting step in.

An emergency fund is just a stash of money set aside only for surprises. Not boring adult stuff like car repairs (okay, maybe that for teen drivers), but also things like a cracked phone screen right before finals or losing your headphones the week of a big group project. Say your bus card stops working and you have to pay for rides, or you need to chip in for a family emergency. When you have a backup fund, you can avoid relying on friends for a loan, begging your parents, or selling your belongings at the last moment to cover a basic fix. Even $20 between you and disaster can keep things from blowing up.

Some people think you need a giant pile of cash before it counts as an emergency fund, but that's not true. Even a small cushion makes a huge difference. Having a backup plan is key to avoiding embarrassment and rash decisions. Your backup shouldn't feel impossible. It should feel like real protection that grows little by little.

Getting your emergency fund started can be pretty direct. If you get birthday or holiday money from relatives, you can put aside a small chunk, maybe $10 right away. When you have a part-time job or babysit, decide to save just a couple bucks per week, even if that's $2 or $3 at first. Have old video games, jeans, or sneakers you never use? Sell them online or to friends and add that cash to your fund. The secret is to start with amounts that feel realistic and hit those early wins: aim for $20, see how it feels. Next, try for $50. Once you hit $100, you'll realize you can actually crush bigger challenges too.

Motivation makes all the difference. Some people like tracking their savings progress with a fun chart on their wall or a private note on their phone. Others set a silly or inspiring name for their fund, like "Break in Case of Drama" or "Peace of Mind Jar." Celebrate when you reach mini-goals by letting yourself feel good, not by raiding the fund, but by telling someone, treating yourself to a movie at home with snacks, or just marking the achievement.

Thinking about the next layer, saving isn't just reacting to problems. It's about designing your own future, so the stuff you want isn't only a wish. Short-term goals might be a new video game, upgrades for your bike, or going out for pizza with friends. Long-term goals are bigger things, maybe buying your first car, putting money toward a college laptop, or saving for a trip you actually care about. The big difference? Short-term goals are a month or two away, while long-term goals need a bunch of smaller steps over a year or more.

The best way to make goals happen is to be real about them. Ask yourself, what do I actually see myself doing or having that would make me proud? List these goals somewhere safe. Once you know them, making a plan is easier. Instead of feeling like you need $300 for a concert ticket all at once, break it down. Saving

$5 a week for four months gives you $80. Need $180 for a trip? That's $15 a month for a year.

Sample Savings Milestones

Savings Plan	1 Month	3 Months	4 Months	6 Months	8 Months	12 Months
Save **$5 per week**	$20	$60	–	$120	–	–
Save **$15 per month**	–	–	$60	–	$120	$180

Sometimes, the big goals or random emergencies can feel like too much. It's totally normal to get overwhelmed or want to spend instead. Get around this by focusing just on the next small step. If your goal is saving $100, focus on the first $10, repeat until you hit the next bump. Remind yourself why you wanted this fund or goal in the first place (write it on a sticky note or make it a phone wallpaper). Loop in a friend, so you keep each other on track or have a little competition. Try making a challenge, see who can save $30 the fastest, or who skips takeout for two weeks.

Once you've got the basics down, saving can actually get way easier. There are simple tools and tricks that let you build your fund or hit your goal without even thinking, almost by autopilot. Next, it's time to look at ways to make saving effortless, no matter what your budget or personality.

Making Saving Effortless: Automation and Practical Steps for Any Budget

You already set some goals for your savings and stuck with emergency funds, so how do you actually make those dreams happen without feeling broke? The secret lies in your habits. Daily actions matter more than big promises. It's not about hoping you'll remember to save but setting things up so you save without thinking. That makes reaching a savings target way easier, even if you don't have much income coming in or if your spending always seems to change with every week.

You don't have to force yourself to make tough decisions every time you get paid. Automation takes over and does the work for you. Online banking apps make it pretty simple. One easy strategy: schedule a transfer to your savings account the day after you get paid. Maybe you earn $25 from a weekend shift or someone CashApps you for walking their dog. Instead of waiting or telling yourself you'll save "later," arrange a recurring transfer through your banking app. Most banks work like this:

1. Open your banking app and find the "Transfer" or "Move Money" section.
2. Pick how much you want to move, from your checking to your savings account. Even $1 counts.
3. Choose "Repeat" or "Schedule," and pick a set date (like payday, or every Saturday).
4. Save the settings, and you're set. The app will now move money behind the scenes, instantly, with no extra thought.

Banking apps constantly add new features to make this easier. Some now offer "round-up" programs. If you use a debit card, every time you buy something the app rounds up the purchase to the next dollar and sends the spare change to your savings. Buy a smoothie for $4.20? The app tucks away $0.80 for you. Over a week, those tiny extras add up.

Here's a week-in-the-life story: Imagine Riley, who works shifts at a fast food place and uses a debit card for snacks and bus rides.

Riley turns on the bank's "round-up" feature through the app. On Monday they grab a coffee ($2.70, a $0.30 round-up). On Tuesday, they buy fries for $3.40 (another $0.60 saved). Each day, the spare change goes to savings, and by Friday, Riley checks the app and sees $4.50 saved, without once choosing to "cut back." It doesn't feel like less money in Riley's pocket, but those coins turn into a few dollars fast.

Some prepaid cards let you make savings "buckets." You can have your "Withholdings" bucket (emergency fund) and your "Dream Trip" bucket. When you load your card with gift money or pay from a side gig, drag a dollar or two into each bucket. Some apps, like Greenlight or Step, let you split funds and even set saving goals, showing your progress as a bar chart, which turns saving from a chore into a game.

Even if your income bounces all over the place, you can still build up savings. Try the "pay yourself first" trick. The second you get any money, put a dollar straight into savings, even before you do anything else. Only one dollar? That's fine. The habit beats the amount. If you don't notice $1 leaving each week, you bank $52 in a year, enough for concert tickets or late-night pizza runs when you need them. If you pick up a few babysitting gigs or sell old clothes, treat each "bonus" as a savings chance, stash $3 from every $20, or the leftover change from selling sneakers. Gift money counts too.

Alerts and reminders can help if an app doesn't do automation. Most banking and budgeting apps let you turn on notifications. Set up a calendar reminder labeled "Save $1" on payday or each Sunday. When the alert pops up, transfer what you have, even if it's just spare change.

Saving isn't about denying yourself fun or splurging now and then. It means you always have your own back. A small savings stash means you can pay for a day trip to the city, jump on a friend's movie invite, or buy extra phone data when everyone else's WiFi is down. Every dollar saved today boosts your freedom and lowers stress in the future, and you don't have to nail it every week; consistency beats perfection. Saving $1 a day adds up to $30 in a month. That's a new hoodie or extra streaming for your crew. Skip some days? You'll still have something waiting when you need it. It's your money, working for you; you just gave yourself a little more power and choice.

Now that you understand how saving even small amounts can build your freedom and confidence, it's time to put these simple strategies into action. Whether it's setting up automatic transfers, rounding up purchases, or starting an emergency fund with pocket change, every step you take brings you closer to having real control over your money. Saving isn't about missing out; it's about making sure you're ready for whatever pops up and giving yourself the power to say yes to the things that matter most. Keep it steady, keep it realistic, and watch as your savings grow into something that supports your goals and your future. You've got this!

CHAPTER 5
SMART SPENDING
HOW TO STOP WASTING YOUR MONEY

"Wait, did I really just spend ten bucks on a game upgrade? And another five on snacks today?" You scroll through your bank app, squinting at the numbers and wondering where all your money went. It's not like you blew your whole paycheck on one big thing; those small buys sneak up on you: a coffee here, a streaming subscription you forgot to cancel there, a last-minute impulse click online. Suddenly, your balance looks way smaller than you expected, and it feels like your cash is disappearing without you noticing.

It happens to almost everyone, especially when life gets busy and spending becomes automatic. Maybe you weren't even hungry but grabbed a snack out of habit, or maybe an ad popped up on your feed just when you were bored, urging you to hit "buy now." Sometimes it's hard to tell if that new hoodie or those earbuds are something you really want or just a shiny distraction. These moments add up, leaving you puzzled and frustrated about your money.

But what if you could hit pause before these little purchases? What if you learned how to catch those sneaky reasons behind your spending and take back control? Imagine feeling confident about every dollar you spend, knowing it lines up with what really matters to you. That kind of control doesn't come from magic. It comes from noticing patterns and making choices on purpose, not on autopilot.

The road to smart spending isn't about cutting out all fun or treats; it's about learning to see where money slips away and understanding why those impulses happen. It's about spotting ads and social media tricks designed to push you toward buying things you might regret. And most importantly, it's about shifting from wandering through your spending to deciding where your money goes.

If you've ever felt confused by your bank statements or wondered how to stop wasting cash on stuff that doesn't last, this chapter is for you. It's a chance to start thinking differently about your money, so your future self can thank you for every smart choice you make today.

Identifying Costly Habits and Spending with Purpose

It's easy to wonder where your paycheck went when just last week it felt like you had plenty in your account. Maybe you've sat in class, hungry after lunch, and Venmo'd a few dollars for pizza or energy drinks. Or you noticed a charge from a streaming service you barely use, buried in your bank app, and remembered you'd meant to cancel that free trial months ago. A late-night boredom scroll can end with "Buy Now" on a game upgrade or extra hoodie. None of these choices seem like a big deal on their own, but after a few weeks, the little expenses pile up and leave your balance looking much lower than expected.

Many teenagers encounter this obstacle and experience frustration. Money just seems to vanish, but it's rarely one single moment or massive purchase. Instead, most people lose money in drips - quick snacks, small cash apps, monthly subscriptions, and last-minute downloads. Some of the spending happens on impulse, maybe because you're feeling stressed or want a quick boost after a tough day. Other times, it comes from habits you picked up without thinking, like grabbing boba tea out of routine, not because you really want it that day.

Common Money Leaks

It helps to put a spotlight on where money leaks actually happen. Here are a few places to check for sneaky spending:

- **App subscriptions**: photo editing tools, streaming platforms, or games that auto-renew each month
- **Quick snacks or drinks**: daily coffee runs, vending machine treats, drinks after practice
- **Boredom buys**: online shopping when you're bored or overwhelmed, even if the item isn't needed
- **In-app purchases**: game upgrades or customizations that add up over time
- **Impulse group spends**: chipping in for repeated fast-food runs with friends
- **Forgotten free trials**: services you no longer use that charge automatically after a trial period

Spotting these leaks means noticing patterns in your day-to-day life, not just focusing on one big moment.

Spotting Leaks: Explanation of method or task

The best way to know where your money is slipping away is a quick money review. This exercise isn't about feeling bad. The goal is to figure out where your money actually goes so you can make it work for you.

Detailed steps for the method or task

1. **Open your bank or payment app**: Look at your transaction history from the past month.
2. **Highlight recurring charges**: Mark any subscription or monthly payment. These are easy to forget since they leave your account on their own.
3. **Circle daily or weekly repeats**: Maybe it's a favorite snack or something you buy out of habit. Look for patterns.
4. **Notice in-the-moment spends**: Go through purchases that felt like "no big deal" at the time. These are usually under $10, but together, they matter.
5. **Write down what you find**: Make a simple list or talk through your findings with someone you trust - a parent, sibling, or friend. Pick honesty over shame. Everybody has leaks; the goal is to spot them.

In the next part of this chapter, we'll take a closer look at how ads and social media influence your decisions, so you'll be ready to spot those tricks and keep control of your cash.

From Drifting to Deciding

Once you know where your money is escaping, taking control becomes possible. Setting small, clear goals for your spending makes a big difference. If you want to save $20 for a tech upgrade or only eat out two Fridays a month, write it down where you can see it. Simple, realistic targets give you something to aim for, making your spending feel less random and more in your hands.

Letting go of automatic spending happens when you make each choice on purpose. Before hitting buy, pause and ask yourself, "Will I still care about this next week?" or "Would I rather use this money for something bigger?" Make a shopping list before you go out, so you don't end the day buying stuff you forgot you already have. If you're tempted between two good things, like downloading a new game or adding that money toward savings for a concert, you suddenly see that every dollar has options.

Values-Based Spending

Spending with intention gets easier when you match your habits to what matters most. This means checking if your money lines up with your values. Think about the three things you care about most like creativity, friendship, or independence. Next, look back at your spending: where did your money go last month? Jot down your top values, then make a quick list of your biggest expenses. See if the two lists line up.

If you love art but haven't spent money on any supplies or experiences in weeks but have bought snacks or trendy gear out of habit, that's something to notice. It's not about being perfect; it's about making your money start to support the things you actually care about. This self-check can give you new ideas and renewed motivation to shift your habits, helping you feel positive about how you spend, save, and share your money going forward.

Recognizing Manipulation: Ads, Social Media, and Value Judgment

Imagine this: you're just relaxing, flipping through Instagram, and suddenly a sponsored post pops up. It shows off the latest sneakers, worn by your favorite YouTuber, who casually says, "Just got these—love them!" Right after, a story flashes by with a countdown: "ONLY 2 HOURS LEFT for 30% off!" You find yourself looking for those sneakers, wondering if you have enough saved up. Scenarios like these happen every day, and they're not accidents. Companies and influencers have learned how to tap into the feelings that make you want to act fast before you have time to ask, "Do I actually need this?"

The world of advertising today is more than billboards and TV commercials. Ads now pop up everywhere you go online, powered by all the data you leave behind. If you've noticed an ad following you from one app to another or felt like something on your phone was "reading your mind," you're experiencing targeted advertising in action. These companies track what you like, who you follow, and even what you've scrolled past. They use this data to serve ads they think will reach you at the right time.

The tricks don't stop there. Advertisers and influencers are masters at using FOMO - the fear of missing out. They use countdown timers, tags like "just dropped," and phrases like "selling out fast" or "don't miss out." These get your heart racing. The goal is to make you feel as if a delay could mean you'll lose out forever. Social media only ramps things up, because you see what your friends and idols are sharing or buying, and it's easy to think, "Maybe I should have that, too." Sometimes, a post looks like a genuine recommendation, but really, it's a paid partnership designed to make you want what they're selling.

Here's what's happening in your brain during all this: when you see something that triggers excitement, your mind releases chemicals that make you feel good. That "rush" can make it hard to pause and think things through. Suddenly, a purchase feels urgent and necessary, even if you were fine five minutes before. It's like someone pushing a big, shiny "buy now" button inside your head.

Spotting these tricks isn't always easy, but you can train yourself to notice. Try this: look at your feed and keep an eye out for words and phrases meant to amp up excitement or urgency. These include "must-have," "only a few left," and "get yours while you can." If you see a product pop up again and again, maybe different people mention it, or you keep seeing it in ads, make a quick note in your phone. Ask yourself: is this a real recommendation, or just a clever ad in disguise?

A conversation might go like this in your mind:

"Wow, this influencer I follow just said these headphones are the best thing ever."

But then: "Wait, didn't they say last month's headphones were awesome, too?"

Follow that up with: "Are they getting paid to say this? Or do they actually use them?"

Getting more aware of these thoughts is step one. The next part is learning to put each tempting purchase through a test before spending your money.

The Value Check: A Three-Step Method

1. **Usefulness:** Is this something that will make your life better or easier? For instance, will those headphones help you focus during study time, or will they just be another accessory in your backpack?
2. **Durability:** Will the item last? Have you bought things before that felt exciting at first but broke, stopped working, or lost their appeal almost instantly?
3. **Personal Goals:** Does it fit with what you're saving up for or care about most? Maybe you've been dreaming about a summer trip or a new skateboard; pausing to check if this purchase supports that goal helps make sure your money goes where you really want it.

Picture this: you see a hoodie shouted out by a TikTok star, limited edition, flashy colors, and a price that eats up most of this month's allowance. Pause for one minute and walk through the three steps. Will it be your new favorite or just a closet dweller? Compare that to saving for a guitar that'll help you start a band. Suddenly, it's easier to see what lines up with your real plans.

Build Your Skills With This Exercise

1. Screenshot or jot down three things you felt tempted to buy after seeing them on social media or in an ad.

2. For each one, walk through the value check:

- Write if it'll really be useful.
- Think about how long it might last.
- Note if it fits with what you actually want most.

3. Look over your notes; does anything stand out? How many times did a "must-have" turn out to be a maybe, or even a "skip it"?

In Chapter 5, you're learning more than how to spot your spending habits. You're also practicing how to push back when companies or influencers try to drive your choices. Every step makes you more confident and helps you stay in charge—today and with every money decision you'll make in the future.

As you keep practicing, you'll start seeing other smart ways to shop—like finding better prices or picking things that last. The more you use these habits, the more your future self will thank you.

Becoming a Smart Shopper: Quality Over Quantity and the 'Delay, Compare, Decide' Mantra

Smart spending jumpstarts when you learn to spot the sneaky ways ads and trends try to pull you into buying stuff without thinking. Once you notice those tricks, you can flip the script and start making choices that fit your goals, not someone else's playbook. Instead of falling for every must-have gadget or one-day offer, you can focus on what actually matters to you.

We are investing in better items, such as a backpack that won't rip halfway through the year. It helps your money stretch farther. It's easy to get sucked into the excitement of something new, but most cheap things break, fade, or get tossed before long. If you pick a hoodie you wear all year instead of three that go out of style, you're not only saving cash, you're also saying no to closet clutter and waste. Think about earbuds: you might see a flashy pair online for half the price, but if the sound is bad or they die in a month, was it really a deal? Spending once on something solid means less hunting for replacements and more left over for the big stuff.

Impulse shopping creeps in at every corner, especially with the way snacks and gadgets pile up around the checkout or how websites slide in "You might like this, too" at the last second. Maybe you're running an errand for your family, and a candy bar calls your name, or you're scrolling TikTok and see all your friends unboxing the same phone case. Even online, flash sales tempt you to buy before you "miss out," which ramps up that need to click before thinking. Instead of falling into those traps, try pausing and asking yourself, "Am I buying this because I truly want it or because it's right there, yelling at me?"

One way to skip buyer's regret is to hit pause with the "Delay, Compare, Decide" strategy. Here's how it plays out.

Delay

Don't hand over cash or tap "buy now" right away, even for something you want. Set a 24-hour rule for stuff you don't need urgently. Walk away from the display or close the browser. After sleeping on it, check in with yourself. Is this still worth your hard-earned money, or did the excitement fade? Waiting cools off snap feelings and saves you from loads of purchases you'd regret later.

Compare

If you still want it, turn into a detective. Check out the same item at other stores or sites. Are there versions with better reviews or a sturdier build? Maybe your friend bought one last year and can share what they think. Read comments, star ratings, or even quick social media posts to spot obvious issues or hidden gems. You might find a student discount, a price match, or another brand that gets you more for less.

Decide

Once you've compared, line up what you've learned with your budget. If you're choosing between a burger with friends or saving toward a new skateboard, which will feel better later? Ask what fits your needs (not what an ad or influencer says). Sometimes, the best choice is walking away and saving the money for something you care about more.

Let's say you need new jeans. Your first pick is a trendy brand on sale, but after a quick search, you spot another pair, no fancy logo, but strong stitching, and it's known for lasting. You speak with a friend who owns a pair and finds them comfortable and long-lasting. You decide to save your cash for the second pair, confident you'll actually wear them and they won't end up ripped in a month.

Shopping smart gets easier with a few tips you keep in your back pocket. Here's a checklist to lean on before you buy:

- Write down what you plan to buy. Stick to the list when you hit the store or shop online.
- Choose a spending limit. Don't go over, even if something super tempting pops up.
- Check for deals, student discounts, price matches, or coupons before you buy.
- Never shop when you're bored, worn out, or upset. That's when impulse buys attack the hardest.
- If friends pressure you to buy something just because they did, step back and ask if it's worth it for you, not just for fitting in.

Every dollar you don't waste on stuff you don't love is a step toward bigger dreams, like saving for trips, a car, or college. Think of smart spending as a habit, not just skipping one trip to the mall. You take control of your money when you learn to pause, compare options, and stick to your own goals. This means more freedom, less stress, and confidence every time you say "yes" or "no" at the store. Let your money support you, not control you. That's the start of real financial power.

Now that you know how to spot where your money slips away, recognize the tricks advertisers use, and build smart shopping habits, you're ready to take control of your spending. It's all about making choices that fit what you care about, not just reacting to ads or momentary urges. By pausing before you buy, comparing options, and sticking to your goals, you can stretch your dollars further and feel good about where your money goes. These skills aren't just for today. They set you up to manage your cash confidently as you grow, helping you save for the things that really matter and gain the freedom to make money work for you, not against you.

CHAPTER 6
BANKING 101
WHERE TO KEEP YOUR MONEY SAFE

Most people think keeping money safe just means stuffing cash in a drawer or hiding it under a mattress. But real safety comes from understanding where your money lives, how it moves, and who's watching over it. Imagine handing your hard-earned paycheck to a stranger with no rules. Sounds risky, right? Yet many teens do something similar when they don't know which bank account fits their needs or how debit and credit cards really work.

Knowing these basics isn't just about avoiding mistakes. It's about taking control so your money can grow and support your goals. The good news is that learning how to manage your money safely doesn't have to be confusing or boring. It's about making smart choices that get easier every time you check your balance or swipe your card. This chapter pulls back the curtain on banking and shows you simple steps to protect your cash and build confidence as you start managing your own money.

Types of Bank Accounts and Institutions

It's exciting to start managing your own money, but choosing the right place for it can feel confusing. When you first set up a bank account, you'll notice there are two main types: checking accounts and savings accounts. Each one does a different job for your money, almost like having two pockets, but each with its own rules.

A checking account is built for spending and everyday use. Picture this: you get paid after helping neighbors mow lawns, the money goes straight into your checking account by direct deposit, and you use your debit card to grab pizza with friends or pay for a bus ticket. With checking, you can write checks (if you need to), make online payments, withdraw cash at ATMs, or swipe your card at the store. Most teens like checking accounts because they let you move money around easily, whether that's paying your phone bill, sending funds via your app, or even just keeping your cash in a secure digital wallet instead of a drawer at home.

Savings accounts work differently. Their main purpose is to help you build up cash for things that take longer to save for. Maybe you want to buy a new bike, save for driving lessons, or just have a safety cushion for the future. When your money sits in a savings account, the bank pays you interest, which is like a little "thank you" bonus for not touching your funds right away. Because savings accounts are meant for stashing away funds, you can only take out money a certain number of times per month, this actually helps you avoid spending your savings on impulse. Interest rates are usually better than what you'd get from a checking account, so you grow your money even while you sleep.

Most banks let you connect your checking and savings accounts, so you can move money between the two whenever you need. That means you could split your birthday money, half goes into checking for fun stuff now, and half slides into savings for later goals. You can see everything right in one banking app, manage transfers, set savings goals, and even get notifications when your balance changes.

Comparing these accounts side by side, the benefits of checking are all about access. You can get to your money quickly, link your account to payment apps, and use your debit card almost anywhere. But there's a catch: you usually don't earn much (or any) interest, and you need to watch out for potential fees like overdraft charges—these happen if you spend more than you have in your account. Meanwhile, savings accounts are great for putting your money out of easy reach, so you aren't tempted to spend it right away. They reward patience with higher interest. The main downside is you can't use a savings account to pay for things directly at a café or online; you have to move money to checking first, which takes a little planning.

To see how this fits real life, think about two friends: Mia likes to have her paycheck deposited into checking so she can use her debit card at her favorite store and cover lunch with friends—she checks her balance daily in her app. Josh, on the other hand, splits his allowance between checking and savings. He rarely touches his savings, and is slowly building up enough for concert tickets next summer. These habits show how both account types serve different goals.

Along with picking your first account, you'll also need to choose the kind of bank you want to use. Traditional banks have branches you can walk into, meet with a real person, and ask questions. They offer ATMs and might feel more comfortable if you like talking things through face-to-face. The drawbacks? They sometimes charge more fees for things like low balances or using out-of-network ATMs.

Online-only banks run through apps and websites, without any physical branches. All your customer service happens by chat or phone. Online banks often offer higher interest rates for savings and lower fees, but you can't walk in and ask for help. Depositing checks usually means you snap a photo with your phone, and getting cash requires either using an ATM in their network or transferring money elsewhere. It's all about what feels easiest to you: being able to ask a person for help or always banking from your phone and rarely needing cash.

As you set up your first banking relationship, think about how you spend and save, where you want to get help, and how much you're willing to pay in fees. If you like in-person support, traditional banks might be your pick. If you live on your phone and don't want extra charges, an online bank could be a good fit. No matter which you choose, both checking and savings accounts play a part in keeping your money safe and helping you build habits that last. Debit cards can seamlessly integrate with purchase tracking, and your app will assist you in monitoring every dollar. Getting comfortable with these basics sets you up for smart moves next time you get paid.

Understanding Debit and Credit Cards

After you set up your first checking account, you get access to something that feels kind of powerful: a plastic card with your name on it, ready for real-world spending. This is usually a debit card, and it's worth getting comfortable with how it works before you move on to anything else.

A debit card links straight to your checking account. Every time you swipe, tap, or enter the numbers online, you're paying with your own money. The cash leaves your account almost instantly. Imagine you head to a coffee shop after school and buy a $5 drink with your debit card. Your checking balance drops by $5 right away. Or maybe you use the card at an ATM to grab $20 in cash for a movie night. Again, the balance vanishes in seconds.

Debit cards are popular because they're easy to use and give you a solid grip on your money. If your account holds $50, that's the absolute maximum you can spend—unless your bank allows overdrafts, which means you can accidentally go below zero and owe fees. Most banks set up overdraft protection for a price, so always ask about your settings before you start using your card. With a debit card, you won't end up with a big bill to pay later, the money is only available if you have it.

Pros of Debit Cards

- **Instant spending:** No wait for bills later on. The money leaves your account as soon as you use your card.
- **Easy to control:** It's hard to accidentally spend more than you have, which helps build good habits.
- **Widely accepted:** You can shop or get cash almost anywhere.
- **Security:** Cards come with a PIN number. If you lose your card, call your bank fast so they can block it.

Cons of Debit Cards

- **No credit-building:** Debit cards won't help you start a credit history.
- **Overdraft risks:** Some banks charge a fee if you spend more than you have, unless you set up alerts or turn off overdraft.
- **Limited fraud protection:** If someone steals your card info and drains your account, getting your money back can be harder than with a credit card.

If you lose your debit card, don't panic, but act fast. Call the number on your bank's website to freeze it as soon as you notice it missing. Most banks can give you a new card for a small fee.

Credit cards look and feel like debit cards but play by entirely different rules. When you use a credit card, you're borrowing money from a bank or credit company. You spend now, but you agree to pay the money back in about a month. Suppose you buy concert tickets with a credit card. The charge goes onto your card balance, and at the end of the month you owe the money, plus extra interest if you can't pay it all back right away.

Most teens can't get a credit card on their own until they're at least 18, and sometimes not even then unless they have a job or a co-signer. It can be tempting to jump into credit cards early, but it's often smarter to wait. Building habits with a debit card first helps you learn solid budgeting skills.

Pros of Credit Cards

- **Credit-building:** Every on-time payment boosts your credit score, which is a number (usually 300 to 850) that banks use to predict how trustworthy you are with money.
- **Emergency funds:** If your bike gets stolen and you need a new one, a credit card means you don't have to wait until payday.
- **Extra protection:** If someone scams you online, your credit card company can often erase the charge.

Cons of Credit Cards

- **Risk of debt:** Spend more than you can pay back, and interest builds up fast.
- **Possible fees:** Late payments bring extra charges and hurt your credit score.
- **Not for everyone:** The ability to borrow can make overspending feel too easy.

Debit vs. Credit at a Glance

Card Type	Where Money Comes From	Impacts Credit Score	Can Go Over Limit?	Biggest Risk
Debit Card	Your checking account	No	Overdraft possible	Overdraft fees
Credit Card	Money you borrow	Yes	Yes (bad idea)	Debt + interest

If you're shopping online for sneakers, a debit card keeps things straightforward. The money comes out now, no future bill, but you give up some fraud protection. For booking a trip or hotel, credit cards can offer better safety in case of problems. Still, for most teens, starting with debit is safer. You can't accidentally dig yourself into debt.

Stay on top of things by tracking your balance, setting up alerts for large purchases, and never sharing your card info by text or DMs. Only shop on secure sites (look for "https" in the web address). If you ever find a charge you didn't make, call your bank or credit card company right away.

As you get used to using cards, keeping an eye on your bank account matters even more. Keeping your account safe, using

ATMs smartly, and steering clear of unwanted fees are the next steps to learn on your money journey.

Managing Your Account Safely and Avoiding Pitfalls

Learning how debit and credit cards work opens the door to a whole new world of everyday banking. Once you understand the difference between them, you'll start to see how small choices, like tapping your card for snacks or withdrawing cash, can add up over time. This section explains how to use your bank accounts wisely, avoid common risks, and make confident decisions without stressing over hidden fees or lost money.

ATM Know-How and Safety

Bank accounts work best when you know how to use your money safely, especially when it comes to handling cash. ATMs make it easy to withdraw money without a teller, but a little caution goes a long way. Never share your PIN, even with friends, and always cover the keypad when you type. Check for anything unusual around the card slot, such as extra devices or loose parts, which could be "skimmers" designed to steal your information. If something feels off, walk away and find a different ATM.

ATMs in your bank's network are usually free to use. Once you start using machines from other banks or those in busy spots like gas stations, fees can pile up quickly. You might get charged both by the ATM and by your bank. A couple of out-of-network withdrawals a week can eat into your balance fast. Imagine cashing your first summer paycheck and withdrawing $20 twice from a random machine. After two $3 fees, you've lost $6 just to access your money. Before using an ATM, check your bank's app or website to see if it's part of your network.

Avoiding Overdrafts and Unwanted Fees

Overdrawing your account means you pay with money that isn't there. If you swipe your debit card or set up an auto-payment that exceeds your balance, your bank may cover it, but with a price. Overdraft fees often hit at $30 to $35 per transaction. Buy a milkshake for $4, and that shake might cost five or even ten times as much once you add fees.

It only takes a couple of slip-ups to watch money disappear. Monitoring your finances every few days is the best way to avoid overdraft issues. Use your bank's app to check your balance, and turn on alerts for low funds. Some banks let you get a daily balance text or an alert when spending pushes you close to zero. Keeping a "buffer," say, $20 you never touch, can save you from going negative. Picture this: your Netflix subscription renews automatically on Friday, but you forgot about your midweek snack run. Without tracking, both hit at once, and suddenly you're paying much more for convenience.

Recognizing and Steering Clear of Traps

Banks sometimes tuck fees or rules into the fine print. Teens often trip over monthly maintenance fees or minimum balance requirements. That can mean a $10 or $15 fee each month if your balance dips too low. Some accounts charge for paper statements or if you don't use direct deposit. Auto-payments, like music subscriptions or memberships, can slip off your radar, quietly draining your cash.

A good habit is to review account terms before you sign up or after your first statement. Look for words like "monthly service charge" or "minimum balance." If you can't find the info in the app, type your bank's name and "account fees" into a browser to bring up the details. Make it even easier by setting a reminder on your phone to check for auto-payments once a month.

Opening and Managing Your First Bank Account: Step-by-Step

Starting a new bank account feels like a big leap, but it breaks down into clear steps. Most banks or credit unions want to see a government-issued photo ID (like a driver's license or passport), your Social Security number, and something to prove your address—think a school letter or mail in your name. Many banks need you to bring a parent if you aren't eighteen or if you want a joint account.

In a bank branch, a staff member will explain account choices, walk you through forms, and review the details. You'll set your PIN and can choose extras like mobile alerts. Online, you'll upload digital copies of your docs, tap through the terms, and set up security options. Always read the account rules focus on fees, overdraft terms, and limits. Ask questions, even if they seem obvious. A real example: you finish your summer job, your parent comes with you, and you bring your ID and a paystub. In twenty minutes, you leave with a starter debit card and a shiny new account.

Smart Banking Habits and Real-Life Protection

A few routines boost your safety and peace of mind. Change your online banking passwords every few months and don't reuse them for other sites. Watch out for scams, if you get a "bank" email or text asking to click a link or share info, don't bite. Use your bank's alerts to track withdrawals or deposits and make reviewing your statement a regular thing. These habits stop mistakes before they start, help you catch problems early, and make you the one in control. Over time, being alert makes banking feel safer and saves more of the money you work for.

Now that you understand the basics of banking, from choosing the right accounts and institutions to using debit and credit cards safely, you're ready to take control of your money with confidence. You set yourself up for a strong financial future by monitoring your balances, avoiding unnecessary fees, and developing smart habits early. Whether you prefer a traditional bank or an online app, knowing how to manage your accounts and protect your information means you can handle whatever money situations come your way. This chapter is just the start, next, you'll learn how to make your money work harder for you as you move closer to real independence.

CHAPTER 7
INTRO TO INVESTING
MAKE YOUR MONEY GROW

"Can I really start investing if I'm still in high school and only have a few dollars?" That's the question Mia asked her older cousin one afternoon, sitting on the porch with her phone in hand. Her cousin smiled and said, "You don't need a lot of money or some fancy job to get started. It's all about getting going now, no matter how small." But Mia wasn't so sure. She had seen people on TV talking about stocks and crypto, but it all felt complicated and meant for adults with suits. She wondered if it was really something she could understand or even trust.

Mia's hesitation is something many teens feel when they think about managing money beyond just saving up for the things they want. The idea of investing can seem like a big leap like trying a new game with unknown rules or stepping onto a field you've never played on before. It might feel safer to put that birthday cash straight into your savings jar or spend it on what feels good now. But then there's this quiet thought in the back of your mind: what if doing something small today could actually grow into something much bigger later? What if starting early means more chances to learn, make mistakes, and still come out ahead?

That mix of excitement and uncertainty is where lots of young people find themselves. They want to be smart about money, but they don't want confusing jargon or pressure to have it all figured out from the start. They want to know, simply: who can begin investing, why does timing matter, and how does putting a little bit away now really add up over time? Sometimes just knowing you're not alone in feeling unsure makes it easier to take that first step.

Like learning a new skill, investing doesn't require being perfect right away, in fact, nobody expects you to be an expert on day one. The question isn't about how much money you have to start with, but whether you're ready to take action and see what happens next. It's about building confidence, understanding what's out there, and discovering that growing your money can be something you do, not just something other people talk about.

Investing: Not Just for the Wealthy – Start Small and Think Long-Term

A lot of people believe that investing is only something for rich adults or people who wear suits and watch business news all day. The truth is, anyone can become an investor, even if you're just starting high school or have only a few dollars to your name. Investing is like picking up a new sport or hobby; it might look intimidating from the outside, but you don't need fancy equipment or lots of experience to start. Like a skateboarder learning balance or a chef learning to crack an egg, investing is a skill you build, not a status you're born into.

Think about learning to ride a bike. Nobody expects you to win races on your first try. You grab a helmet, hop on, maybe wobble and fall a few times, and push yourself a little further each day. Investing is like this. You don't need hundreds or thousands in your pocket. Some investment platforms and apps let you begin with pocket change. With apps that support micro-investing, you can get started with as little as $1 or $5, less than what you might spend on a smoothie. These tools are designed to bring everyone along, not just people with piles of extra cash.

Imagine getting $10 for your birthday or $20 for mowing a neighbor's lawn. Instead of spending all of it right away, what if you put $5 aside each week? Over a year, that adds up to $260. When you add a little at a time, the numbers start to climb. Investment apps like Acorns, Stash, or Greenlight let you transfer small sums automatically. This way, you don't need to remember to move money every time you earn. Your investment habit just runs in the background. It's a lot like putting on sunscreen every day. One squirt doesn't seem like much, but over time, those small actions protect you and add up to something meaningful.

Here's a brief look at how this works in practice:

1. Set up an account with a micro-investing app.
2. Link your bank account or debit card.
3. Decide how much to invest each week or month, even if it's just a few dollars.
4. Turn on an automatic transfer to keep things regular.
5. Check in once in a while to see your progress and celebrate hitting goals.

The key isn't how much you put in, but how often. Consistency matters more than size. Much like practicing a musical instrument or pushing yourself to run a little further, steady effort makes a difference. If you invest $5 each week, you'll have $260 after a year, $520 after two, and even more if your investments earn money along the way.

The big secret is that teens have something adults often wish they had: time. In investing, time works like magic. When you put money into an account or fund, it can grow not just from your deposits but from any profits or gains the investment earns. Each year, you might earn some profit, and the next year, you can earn profit on both your original money and your new earnings. This is called compound growth. It's like planting a seed and watching it turn into a small tree, then someday a whole orchard.

Sometimes new investors feel nervous or discouraged. Maybe the market goes down for a while, or you worry about making mistakes. The truth is, even experienced investors face these worries. The best way to build confidence is by sticking to your plan, making steady investments, and not getting panicked by short-term ups and downs. If things feel confusing, learning a little at a time helps. You don't have to know all the terms or strategies to get started. Celebrate each small milestone. Your first automatic deposit, the first time your account balance grows, or setting a new savings target.

Building this habit early makes you someone who is comfortable with money, who can set goals and reach them, and who isn't pushed around by fear. Each step you take, no matter how small, teaches you more than reading about investing ever will. Give yourself permission to feel proud of every dollar put away.

Outside of investments you've heard about on the news or from friends like stocks, index funds, or even cryptocurrencies. There are so many ways to grow your money. Curiosity is your friend here. Learning about what each type means will help you decide which path fits you best. Getting familiar with these options opens up a world where money works for you, not just the other way around.

Basic Investment Options: Stocks, Index Funds, and Crypto Explained

If you ever thought investing was only for rich adults in suits, it's time to see how easy it is to get started. You don't need thousands of dollars or a fancy advisor. You just need a little to begin and the patience to let that money grow over time. Imagine treating your dollars the way you treat the coins left over from lunch, tucking them away, letting them pile up, and watching them turn into something bigger. That's what investment is, and the first step is understanding your options. It's a lot like picking what to do with your birthday money: do you spend it all on one big thing, share it across a couple of cool buys, or try out a digital option your friends are talking about?

Let's break it down with three of the most popular starter choices: stocks, index funds, and cryptocurrency.

Stocks: Tiny Slice of Big Companies

Picture your favorite sneaker brand, a video game company, or a fast-food chain. These companies usually need money to grow, so they offer pieces of themselves called stocks. When you buy a stock, you're buying a tiny ownership piece. Think of it as getting one slice of a pizza. If the company does well, your piece could become worth more, just like a slice of pizza from a famous shop might sell for more if everyone starts craving it. If the company messes up, or people lose interest, that slice could lose value.

Stocks move up and down all the time. One day, a company announces a new product, and its stock price jumps. The next week, some bad news hits, and the price sinks. That's because stock prices depend on what many people think will happen to the company. Teens understand this phenomenon when a new game becomes highly anticipated and everyone desires it, which drives up resale prices; conversely, they also recognize it when a game fails to meet expectations. It's unpredictable, and sometimes you win, sometimes you lose.

You can earn from stocks in two ways:

- If the price goes up and you sell, you pocket the extra.
- Some companies hand out cash to their owners, called dividends. It's like a gamer friend giving you a bonus for helping them win, just for owning part of their team.

But here's the catch: stocks can be risky. Imagine putting all your savings into one game that ends up a total flop. The same can happen with stocks. All your money in one company means you could win big, but you could also lose fast.

Index Funds: The Investment Basket

Now consider an index fund to be a basket that holds lots of slices from lots of pizzas, all at once. Instead of picking one company, you get little bits of hundreds, sometimes even thousands. It's like wanting snacks for a party and buying a variety box instead of betting on one flavor.

Why do people love index funds? Firstly, in the event that one company in the basket experiences a challenging day, the remaining companies could potentially turn things around. Your risk gets spread out. Index funds often follow big lists like the S&P 500, which includes the 500 largest U.S. companies. So when you buy a piece of an index fund, you become a mini-owner of all those companies at the same time.

This approach feels safer and takes less effort. You don't have to know which company will win next, kind of like not needing to guess the popular snack at school, because your basket has a bit of everything. Many beginners use index funds because they make things simpler and less stressful, even if you're not a financial whiz.

Cryptocurrency: Digital Money for a New World

You've probably heard of Bitcoin, maybe on YouTube or TikTok. Cryptocurrency is digital money, coins, or tokens that only exist online. People trade crypto because they hope the value goes up. Bitcoin, Ethereum, and Dogecoin are some examples teens hear about. Unlike stocks, cryptocurrency isn't tied to companies making shoes or burgers. Its price depends on demand, news, and even memes.

Let's say you buy one unit of a cryptocurrency and its value explodes. That has happened for some people. But since there's nothing physical behind it, prices swing wildly. It could skyrocket in a day and crash the next, kind of like a trending TikTok meme that gets old overnight.

Cryptocurrency has a big digital appeal. You don't have to buy through old-school banks. Apps and crypto wallets let you trade any time of day, and some teens find this freedom exciting. But here's what makes it risky: no guarantees, big jumps up and down, and not as much protection if something goes wrong. Imagine spending your birthday cash on the next cool skin in your favorite game, then the game unexpectedly shuts down. That's how quickly things can turn.

Quick Comparison

- **Stocks**: Higher risk, chance for big wins, and also big losses. This requires either research or luck.
- **Index funds**: Lower risk, smaller but steadier returns, great for hands-off investors.
- **Cryptocurrency**: Wild swings, easy to start, but you can lose everything fast.

Story Time

Suppose you've got $100 you want to try investing. Jesse puts $100 into a single stock and wakes up to see it double after a great earnings report. Eliza buys an index fund and sees it grow slowly week by week. Marcus buys crypto, watches it triple overnight, and then it crashes the next day. They all learn something: Jesse gets lucky, Eliza feels steady, and Marcus feels the thrill and the loss.

Each path has risks and rewards. The type you choose depends on how you like to handle surprises. One thing stays true, though: the earlier you start, the more your money can work for you because investments can earn their own profit over time. That's called compounding, and it's what makes small amounts turn into big gains, something you'll read about in the next part.

The Power of Compound Interest

When you first hear the phrase "compound interest," it sounds kind of technical, like some boring adult thing you'll only care about in ten years. But compound interest is one of those real-life superpowers you can actually use, right now, to start building wealth before you've even got your first real job. To see how it works, imagine this: You set aside $100 from a birthday or summer job and decide to try investing it, using one of those index funds or stock apps you read about earlier. You're not some financial genius, just a normal teen making a first move.

Here's the simple idea. Compound interest is what happens when the money you make from your investments starts earning its own money. It's like a snowball rolling down a hill. At first, it looks tiny. Then, as it keeps rolling, it collects more and more snow, growing faster with each turn. In money terms, once your investment starts earning returns (the extra cash from interest, dividends, or market gains), those earnings are added back into your main pile. Then, next year, you earn interest not just on your original $100 but also on the new "snow" you picked up along the way.

To make this real, check out how it works for two teens. Let's call them Alex and Jordan. Alex decides to start investing at age 15, putting in that $100 and never adding another cent. Jordan waits until age 25 to do the same thing. Both of them earn an average return of 8% per year; a pretty realistic number for stocks and index funds over the long haul. Here's how their money piles up, just letting compound interest go to work.

Alex (Starts at 15)

- Year 1: $100 × 1.08 = $108
- Year 5: $100 × (1.08)^5 = about $147
- Year 10: $100 × (1.08)^10 = about $216
- Year 20 (Alex at 35): $100 × (1.08)^20 = about $467
- Year 40 (Alex at 55): $100 × (1.08)^40 = about $2,172

Jordan (Starts at 25)

- Year 1: $100 × 1.08 = $108
- Year 5: $100 × (1.08)^5 = about $147
- Year 10: $100 × (1.08)^10 = about $216
- Year 30 (Jordan at 55): $100 × (1.08)^30 = about $1,006

Even though they both only invested $100, Alex has more than double the money that Jordan does at age 55. This is the power of time. Each extra year you let your money sit, the more it grows, not in a boring straight line, but in big leaps.

What about simple interest? That's the plain version, and it's less exciting. Simple interest only pays you based on your original amount, not on the "snow" you picked up. If Alex had $100 at 8% simple interest for 40 years, it would be:

- $100 × 0.08 = $8 per year
- Over 40 years: $8 × 40 = $320 in interest
- Total: $100 + $320 = $420

But with compound interest, we already saw Alex's money climb to over $2,100. The key difference is this: with simple interest, the pile never gets bigger, just a few bucks at a time. With compound interest, the pile itself gets so big it starts multiplying. Each year, what you made last year joins the team and helps you earn more.

Visualizing compound interest helps. Think of growing a plant. If you just leave it in a tiny pot, it gets bigger at first, but then it stops. Compound interest is like moving the plant into a new pot every year. Every single time the roots get more room, it bursts with more energy. The longer it grows, the bigger it gets, way past what you expected at the start.

This isn't only about putting money in stocks. Whether you choose to use an index fund or invest a small amount in a crypto account with compounding gains, the lesson remains relevant. Time is the booster. Even small amounts matter if you give them plenty of years to grow. You don't have to pick perfect investments or start with a ton of cash. Just starting early and taking action as soon as you can is how people build real wealth, even if they aren't making giant money yet.

The trick is patience and consistency. Allow the process to unfold; avoid pursuing immediate gains. When you check your investment after one year, it might not look mind-blowing. However, if you remain committed, your money will improve its ability to generate more income each year. Learning this as a teen means by the time you're an adult, you already have a head start, no matter what the adults around you did. This is what power over your future looks like, just from understanding and using compound interest.

Now that you understand the basics of investing, who can start, and why starting early matters, you're ready to take your first steps toward making your money work for you. Remember, it doesn't matter how much you begin with—what counts is getting into the habit of investing regularly and letting time do its magic through compound growth. Whether you choose stocks, index funds, or even try a bit of cryptocurrency, the key is staying patient and consistent. By starting now, you're building a strong foundation that can grow throughout your life, giving you more control and confidence over your financial future than most adults ever had. So go ahead, take action today—the sooner you start, the brighter your money's future will be.

CHAPTER 8
CREDIT SCORES, LOANS, AND FUTURE YOU

When Jamie applied for a car loan at 17, it wasn't just about getting wheels. It was the first step toward independence. The bank looked not only at the money but also at Jamie's track record, paying bills on time, managing small responsibilities, and building trust without even realizing it. Meanwhile, Taylor thought that opening a store credit card for discounts was harmless fun, but missed payments later made it harder to secure college housing.

These stories aren't just about loans or credit cards. They're about choices that quietly shape your future. What if you could start making smarter choices now, building habits that open doors instead of closing them? Understanding how credit works, what loans really mean, and how your financial decisions affect your future is like having a map to navigate life's bigger moments. The best part is that you don't have to wait until adulthood to begin.

The Basics of Credit and Its Impact on Your Future

Imagine your best friend asks to borrow twenty bucks to buy a concert ticket. You hand over the money, no problem, but you expect them to pay you back on time, just like they promised. That simple trust, where you believe someone will return what they owe, is at the heart of credit. It's about more than just dollars and cents. Credit is a reputation for keeping promises, and that reputation starts building earlier than most people realize.

Sometimes credit feels like something only adults worry about, but it pops up in teen life, too. Think about signing up for a streaming service or taking over your own phone bill. Instead of paying right away, the company lets you use their service and asks you to pay at the end of the month. That's credit in action. The company trusts you'll keep your word and pay, and if you don't, they might cut off the service or charge you more next time. It works the same when you get a credit card: you can buy things right now, but you promise to pay the card company later. It's easy to mix up paying with debit (which uses money you already have) and using credit (which is money you're borrowing for now).

If you ever plan to move out, buy a car, or even sign up for a college loan, credit becomes a big deal. For example, maybe you want to get your own apartment during college. The landlord usually checks if you have a "credit history," which is a record of how well you've handled borrowing and repaying in the past. Never borrowed money or always missed payments? The landlord might ask for a bigger security deposit or turn you down. On the other hand, a solid credit history can mean an apartment is yours, with fewer obstacles.

When you get older and start thinking about buying a car, the dealership or lender will look at your "creditworthiness," basically how risky it would be to lend you money. If you've always paid your credit card bills on time and kept your balances low, you've sent a message that you're responsible. The reward might be a lower interest rate, which means you pay less in the long run. But let's say you got a credit card at eighteen and missed payments or always owed a lot. Those habits show up, too, and lenders might offer you smaller loans at higher costs or might say "no thanks" altogether.

Here's a story that many teens will face: Jamie, age 17, wants to buy a used car for a job across town. Their parents agree to help and suggest Jamie apply for a small auto loan in their name, with a parent as co-signer. Jamie has a part-time job and has paid their phone bill on time for a year but has never had a credit card. The bank looks at Jamie's short credit history and the parent's stronger credit. Because Jamie made payments on time, things look good, and the bank offers a fair interest rate. Now, Jamie gets the car with affordable monthly payments, all because of simple, responsible actions started in high school.

It can also go the other way. Take Taylor, who decided to open a loyalty card for the store at the mall to get a 20% discount. At first, it felt awesome to buy new clothes with no cash up front. But Taylor forgot to pay the bill three months straight. When it came time to move into a college apartment, the landlord checked Taylor's credit history and noticed those late payments. The landlord asked for a much bigger deposit, making the whole move-in process extra stressful.

Every choice to borrow money, pay a bill on time, or skip a payment leaves a mark on your credit record. Good habits, such as charging only what you can afford and always paying on time, can lead to opportunities in the future, such as obtaining the best rates on loans or navigating through an apartment application process. Messy habits, like paying late or maxing out a credit card, lead to headaches, higher costs, and missed opportunities. The best part? Starting early, even with small steps, makes the whole system work for you rather than against you.

One surprise for many teens is that their credit reputation is being tracked and scored. Whether you have a simple phone bill or your first credit card, the way you handle these accounts ends up on a report. Soon enough, you might hear the term "credit score." That number becomes a kind of grade for how you handle money, and knowing how it works, and how to protect it, is the next piece you'll want in your financial toolkit.

How Credit Scores Work and Building Strong Habits Early

Getting the hang of credit scores is almost like learning the grading scale at school, only instead of math tests or English essays, you're measured on the way you borrow and repay money. Every person who starts using credit gets a number, usually between 300 to 850, that tells lenders if you're reliable, risky, or somewhere in between. You can think of a credit score as your financial GPA. Just like a strong GPA opens doors to good colleges, a stronger credit score can get you more freedom for things like apartment hunting, snagging the phone plan you want, or saving real money when you want to buy a used car.

A score isn't random; it's made up of several main parts. The first and most important is payment history. Imagine you always turn in homework on time, teachers know they can count on you. Lenders feel the same when you pay your bills by the due date, whether it's a credit card, loan, or even a phone bill. Every time you pay late, it's like missing an assignment, and your score can take a hit. It usually takes the longest to recover from late payments, so catching up quickly when life gets busy really helps.

Another big factor in your credit score is how much debt you are carrying right now. If you use a credit card, the closer your balance is to your credit limit, the more it looks like you are overloaded. Think of it like carrying a backpack full of books all day. It is heavy, and people might wonder how much more you can handle. Using less than a third of what is available to you, or even better, only buying what you can pay off at the end of the month, gives you more flexibility and shows lenders that you are in control.

The length of your credit history is a quieter but still important part of the picture. It shows how long you have been proving that you can handle credit responsibly. Opening your first credit card or becoming an authorized user on a parent's card starts the credit clock. Just like in class, where your teacher gets to know your work habits over time, steady and positive behavior improves your score the longer you keep it up.

How often you apply for new credit also matters. Each time you apply for a new card, loan, or payment plan, a lender checks your credit score. This is called a hard inquiry. One or two checks now and then are fine, but opening several accounts too close together can make lenders nervous. They might think you are struggling financially or taking on too much at once.

The types of credit you have also play a role. A healthy mix, such as a credit card, a small personal loan, or a student loan, shows that you can manage different responsibilities. It is like having a schedule full of different subjects in school. Handling a variety of things well is a good sign, but you do not need every kind of credit to build a strong score.

Why does this score matter before you are even old enough to rent your own apartment? Imagine you are signing up for a new cellphone plan, but your score is low because you missed a few store card payments. You will probably have to pay a higher deposit, leaving you with less money for other things. Later, when you are ready to share rent with friends, a stronger score could save you from paying extra fees or needing someone to guarantee your payments. If you decide to buy a car, a better score can mean a lower interest rate, which can save you hundreds of dollars over time.

Forgetting a payment, ignoring a small bill, or leaving a credit card unpaid might seem like a small mistake, but these slip-ups can lower your score and cost you more money in the long run. Keeping track of your credit and staying consistent with payments helps you build trust, and that trust opens doors when you need it most.

A great way to build good habits from the start is to try a few self-help challenges. Imagine getting your first credit card. First, set a reminder on your phone or in a planner a few days before your payment is due each month. Next, check your card balance online twice a month. If your spending starts to climb, adjust it before it hurts your score. At least once a year, use a free credit report tool online to look for mistakes or unusual charges. Errors can happen, and catching them early can save you a lot of trouble. As you practice these steps, write down what feels difficult. Do you forget due dates? Is tracking your spending frustrating? Talk it through with friends, ask family for advice, or use digital tools to make each habit easier. The earlier you begin these routines, the more natural they will feel over time.

Having these habits makes a big difference when new opportunities appear. Maybe you are ready to buy your first car and the dealership checks your score. If you have managed your credit well, you can qualify for a loan with a fair interest rate that fits your budget simply because you turned financial habits into everyday actions. When you treat your credit score with the same focus you give to school, sports, or hobbies, you are building real independence and freedom for whatever comes next.

Borrowing Wisely: Navigating Loans and Understanding Debt Types

Getting comfortable with credit opens the door to some of life's bigger steps, like buying your first car, getting into college, or handling everyday purchases safely. A strong credit score and smart financial habits make borrowing feel way less scary and way more in your control. When you're ready to take out a loan or use a credit card, knowing what you're really signing up for can make your choices feel smarter, not just riskier.

Student Loans, Car Loans, and Credit Cards

Think of student loans as money you borrow to pay for college or trade school. Imagine you get accepted to your dream school and realize your part-time job or savings are not enough to cover the full cost. That is where a student loan helps. The basic idea is that you borrow a certain amount, called the principal, and agree to pay it back over time with interest. Interest is the extra money the lender charges you for borrowing from them. For example, if you borrow ten thousand dollars at a five percent annual interest rate, you will owe more than that by the time you finish paying it off, depending on how long repayment takes.

Now let's look at car loans. Suppose you need a car for a new job but do not have enough saved yet. A car loan lets you buy the car now and pay for it gradually, with interest added. You will see terms such as monthly payment, which is how much you pay each month; principal, which is the amount you borrowed; and interest rate, which is the percentage charged on top. For instance, if your car loan is eight thousand dollars with a six percent interest rate for four years, you will make a fixed payment each month until both the loan and the interest are paid in full.

Credit cards work a little differently. They act as a flexible type of loan that you can use up to a certain limit and pay back on your own schedule. If you buy one hundred dollars of items with a credit card and do not pay the full balance by the end of the month, interest is added to what remains. Minimum payments are the smallest amount you can pay to keep your account in good standing, but paying only the minimum means you will carry the debt longer and end up paying much more overall.

What to Know Before You Owe

Borrowing isn't just about getting the money you need right now. It's also about future you. Whenever you fill out a loan application or sign up for a credit card, stop and ask yourself these questions:

- How much will you really pay in total, including interest?
- Are you sure you can handle the monthly payments, even if your job hours get cut or you have new expenses?
- If you miss a payment, what are the consequences? Will you pay late fees or see your credit score drop?
- How does this debt fit into your future plans? Does it build you up, or make life harder down the road?

Imagine buying your first car to drive to your after-school job. The loan seems doable, but then your car breaks down and you need to pay for repairs, or you lose some hours at work. Will you still be able to make your payments, plus cover new bills? If you can't, late payments might show up on your credit report, making it tougher to borrow for bigger things (like an apartment or house) later.

If you're thinking about a student loan, ask if the jobs you'll qualify for after graduation will help you pay off that debt. For credit cards, ask if you need to use them for safety (shopping online without cash) or if you're just tempted to buy things you don't really need.

Good Debt Versus Bad Debt

Not all debt is the same. Some can actually give you a boost. College loans can be worth it if your degree leads to a better job or higher paycheck. That's good debt: it grows your potential. Bad debt usually comes from high-interest credit cards when you buy things you don't truly need, and then struggle to pay off the balance, racking up interest each month. If the debt makes your life harder or only offers temporary happiness, that's a red flag.

Before borrowing, ask: "Will this loan or credit make my future brighter, or just cost me more in the end?" If it helps you earn more or get somewhere important (like school or work), it might be worth it. If it's just for a quick thrill or impulse purchase, think twice.

Making Wise Borrowing Choices

There are ways to make smarter borrowing choices. Compare loan offers. One lender's interest rate can be much lower than another's, saving you money. Don't rush into "instant approval" credit cards at the mall or online. Read any offer closely, and don't be afraid to ask questions. If you're confused, ask someone you trust or a financial professional for advice.

A strong credit score doesn't just help you get approved. It can mean lower interest rates and fewer fees. For example, if your friend gets a car loan and you both borrow $6,000, but your strong credit earns you a 4% rate while your friend gets 7%, you'll pay hundreds less over the life of the loan. Being careful and asking questions up front pays off for future you.

Now that you understand how credit works, why managing loans wisely matters, and how your choices today shape your financial future, you're ready to take control of your money. Building good habits early like paying bills on time and borrowing only what you can handle can open doors to opportunities like renting your own place, driving your first car, or paying for college without stress. Remember, every smart decision you make adds up to stronger credit and more freedom down the road. So keep learning, stay curious, and use what you've learned here to build a money story that works for you, not against you.

CHAPTER 9

MONEY MISTAKES TO AVOID (BECAUSE THEY HAPPEN!)

Emma's phone buzzed with another group chat message inviting her to the latest pizza hangout after school. She glanced at her balance and knew she only had a few dollars left until her next allowance, but the pressure to join in tugged hard. Earlier that week, she'd promised herself she'd save more, yet somehow the urge to keep up with friends and not miss out kept winning. By the time the weekend rolled around, Emma found herself scrambling to cover small costs she hadn't planned for and wishing she'd been a little more careful. Money mistakes like these sneak up on almost everyone, especially when everyday choices pile together faster than you realize. Recognizing those slip-ups is the first step toward taking control before they spiral out of hand.

Spotting Common Money Traps: Overspending, Under-Saving, and Ignoring Debt

Shopping with friends after school, scrolling through endless feeds of new products, or spotting the latest limited-edition sneakers are all easy ways for money to slip away. It usually starts small, like grabbing a fancy drink or deciding you absolutely need that cool in-game skin right now. Many teens get caught up in these moments, wanting what feels fun, popular, or socially rewarding. The line between needs and wants can blur quickly. Paying for a new game or the newest pair of headphones can suddenly feel more important than saving for something you will actually use for a long time. What starts as a five dollar coffee can easily turn into twenty by the end of the month, money that could have gone toward a bigger goal instead.

A lot of teens promise themselves they will save next time, thinking a small splurge is just a one time treat. But those "just this once" moments add up faster than expected. If you take time to track where your money goes, you might be surprised by how much ends up on wants instead of needs like transportation, school supplies, or your phone bill. Wants are not bad; everyone deserves to have fun and treat themselves. The problem begins when short term spending takes over and stops you from reaching long term goals. It becomes even harder to resist when trends change constantly and temptation appears every time you open an app or walk past a store.

Overspending and How to Spot It

Before buying something, ask yourself if it is a want or a need. Try making a list of what you must have this week to get by, such as bus tickets, lunch, or a new notebook. Then make another list of things that tempt you, like collectibles, fast food meals, streaming upgrades, or trending accessories. Keeping these lists separate, even in your phone's notes app, helps you see where your money really goes and which purchases actually matter. Some teens use helpful tricks, like setting their phone wallpaper to their savings goal, such as a photo of concert tickets, a dream trip, or a driver's license, as a quick reminder before making an impulse buy.

The Pitfall of Under-Saving

Putting off saving seems harmless at first. You might think, "I'll save once my next allowance comes in," or "I don't really need to worry about money until I'm older." The problem is that the future sneaks up faster than you think. A last-minute text about a group concert, a phone that suddenly needs repairs, or an unexpected team fee can pop up without any warning. If your savings are empty because of past small spending, you're left scrambling. This often leads to borrowing, missing out, or having to ask a parent for a "loan" once again.

It's not fun to say no to yourself now, but it's a solid feeling to have enough saved when something you care about comes up. A simple way to start is to save a fixed amount or percentage of every paycheck, birthday gift, or allowance. Putting $5 or even $1 aside regularly is still progress. If you set up automatic transfers to savings (most banks and apps allow this), you won't even miss the money. Seeing that balance grow feels good and makes you less likely to touch it for quick wants.

Ignoring Debts and Letting Them Grow

Borrowing from a friend, using a buy-now-pay-later app, or letting a part-time job's uniform fee slide for weeks can seem like minor issues. The temptation is to put off paying things back because the amounts look small and you feel you have time. Yet, those tiny debts add up fast. If you forget you owe money, or ignore reminders, your reputation can take a hit as can your relationships. It gets awkward always being "the one who hasn't paid back" or having your parents start refusing front money for rides or events.

Not paying debts on time sometimes leads to late fees, or you could even lose access to work shifts, subscriptions, or apps you use every day. A helpful habit is to make a simple list on paper, in your Notes app, or even with calendar reminders about what you owe, when it's due, and to whom. If you can't pay on time, honest communication goes a long way. Just saying, "I'm on it, I'll pay you back Friday after my shift," builds trust and can prevent tension.

Growing Awareness, Feeling in Control

A lot of teens fall into these mistakes because they're reacting out of routine or because no one taught them the real consequences. Recognizing your spending patterns, thinking twice about why you buy, and tracking even small debts gives you the power to choose what really matters. These skills don't just fix your money. They help you feel more in control. There's more at play, though. Fitting in, keeping up with friends, or wanting what's showing up in your feed can be even stronger motivators than you think when it comes to money choices.

The Power of Peer Pressure: How FOMO and Financial Comparison Shape Your Choices

After learning about the usual money traps, it's worth thinking about what makes them so tempting in the first place. It's one thing to know you should save, avoid racking up credit card debt, or think before buying. Yet every day, there's something that makes even the strongest plans feel shaky. For a lot of teens, that "something" is usually other people—friends, social media, and the feeling that everyone is just a little ahead when it comes to having stuff or doing cool things.

Why Peer Pressure, FOMO, and Comparison Hit So Hard

You walk into the cafeteria, sit down with your friends, and within five minutes, plans for the weekend are buzzing around the table. Someone suggests pizza delivery after school and then everyone wants in. Maybe you already spent your allowance or you're saving up for the concert next month, but there's pressure to go along. It's not always direct. Sometimes everybody just acts like ordering takeout is the obvious thing to do, and nobody says, "You have to join," but it still feels almost impossible to say no.

Peer pressure isn't just about friends telling you to spend money. Sometimes, it's smaller things, like feeling awkward when you're the only one not buying popcorn at the movies or not having the latest phone when everybody is posting selfies with brand-new tech.

FOMO, or Fear of Missing Out, is just as powerful as any sale or discount. Maybe you scroll through your feed and see classmates hanging out at a trendy bubble tea spot, and you wonder if you missed an invite. Or every day there seems to be a new must-have item such as limited edition sneakers, the latest hoodie, or tickets to a show everyone is talking about. You see how excited everyone else is, and suddenly not having those things feels much bigger than it did five minutes ago. Instead of thinking about what you truly want or need, the fear of being left out pushes you to spend, even when you know your budget is tight.

Social comparison happens quietly, but it can be one of the hardest influences to recognize. When people post pictures of new shoes, gadgets, or fun outings, it is easy to feel like you are the only one not spending or living it up. Even if you were proud of saving for something important, seeing other people's highlight reels can make it tempting to ditch your plan just to keep up. That pressure often leads to impulse shopping or borrowing money for things you do not really need.

How This Messes with Good Decisions

It is common to promise yourself, "I will not spend more than twenty dollars this weekend," only to find yourself broke by Sunday night because everyone decided to go to a movie, grab dinner, and stop by the arcade. The logical part of your brain steps aside when you start worrying about fitting in or missing out. Most people make quick buying decisions based on emotion instead of reason, and social pressure can make that even harder to control.

- A friend posts about scoring a new limited-edition hoodie. You didn't even want one before, but suddenly you're clicking "add to cart."
- Someone tags you in a group DM planning a birthday dinner at a pricey restaurant. Even with a shrinking bank balance, you feel like you have to say yes or risk looking like you don't care.
- TikTok floods your feed with viral challenges, like the "no-spend challenge" that somehow requires buying aesthetic journals or apps to track your progress. The trend flips around and turns saving money into just another reason to shop.

When so much of your life is online, seeing others out and about, buying things, or showing off upgrade after upgrade leads to second-guessing your choices. It becomes tough to remember what you actually want versus what looks fun in the moment.

Standing Up to Spending Pressure

While these influences are real, there are ways to protect your money and confidence at the same time.

- Set a spending plan: Decide what you're comfortable spending before you're with friends or scrolling online. Try dividing your allowance or paycheck into goals, some for saving, some for fun, and some set aside just in case.
- Use a cool-off period: If you want something because everyone else has it, set a 24-hour pause before buying. Often, the urge fades and you'll realize you're happier saving for something meaningful.
- Suggest cheaper hangouts: Invite friends to a park, host a movie night at someone's house, or meet up with homemade snacks. Chances are, others feel the pinch too but need someone to speak up.
- Be honest: Saying you're saving for something big, and can't splurge on every outing, shows self-respect, not "boring" energy. You might inspire your friends to be more mindful, too.
- Keep social media in perspective: Remember, everyone posts what they want people to see, not the full story. Follows and likes don't show the real cost, financial or emotional.

Standing your ground gets easier with practice. Real self-respect comes from deciding for yourself, not matching what everyone else does with their money. Slip-ups will happen, and that's normal. What matters is what you do afterward, and how you keep building smarter habits day by day.

Bouncing Back: How to Recover from a Money Mistake Without Freaking Out

Pressure to keep up with trends or not miss out on what friends are doing can sneak into almost any money decision. Even teens who keep close track of their earnings and spending sometimes stumble when everyone around them shows off new stuff or talks up events that cost more than planned. These moments pile on stress, and it's easy to feel alone when a debit card gets overdrawn or a payment is late. Still, the reality is everyone trips up with money from time to time. Dwelling on embarrassment only makes things worse, so the real move is shifting from worry or shame to getting curious and tackling the problem head-on.

Mistakes with money can feel huge in the moment but are nearly always fixable. Ignoring what happened has a way of making the problem grow behind the scenes, so the first step is always the toughest: face it straight on. Open up your banking app or look at a recent statement, even if it means seeing a negative number or a surprise fee. Getting a clear view of what actually happened helps break down that first wall of panic. There may be an overdraft charge for spending a few dollars more than you had, or maybe a forgotten subscription just pulled money from your balance. If you feel a rush of annoyance or panic, that's normal, but don't let it stop you from finding out all the details.

Once the facts are in front of you, it's time to slow down and ask yourself a few questions. What exactly led to this situation? Did a group chat make you feel like a certain online purchase was "mandatory"? Was there a special day or event you gave in to without really thinking about your limit? Or were you simply bored, tired, or distracted when you said yes to something outside your budget? Looking for these triggers can turn a lousy moment into a real learning tool, since knowing what set you off gives you a better shot at dodging the same pitfall next time.

After understanding what happened, move to action. If you've spent too much, could you pause your spending for a couple of days or a week? Maybe check on whether any of the items can be returned, or see if a subscription can be cancelled for a refund. For overdraft or late fee problems, contacting your bank, sometimes with a parent's help, can set things right quicker than expected. Many banks are willing to forgive a first-time fee if you call and ask politely. If your situation involves someone else's money, like borrowing from a friend or your parents, being honest about what happened and walking them through your plan to make things right will almost always go over better than hiding it. Mistakes sting a lot less when you treat them as normal and talk honestly.

Learning to communicate with parents or trusted adults can take some courage, but there's a huge benefit. Trying to cover up a problem often leads to more costs, more stress, and sometimes damaged trust if the mistake gets found out later. On the other hand, bringing up the issue shows maturity and builds trust for bigger financial decisions down the line. Try saying something like, "I messed up my budget last week and went over. Here's what happened, and here's how I'm fixing it." Usually, that approach pulls adults in as problem-solvers, not just people who hand out punishments.

For teens who want structure to help them bounce back, here's one simple exercise that works almost every time:

1. Write down every purchase or expense from the last week or two that led to the problem.

2. Next to each, jot a note about what you were feeling or thinking. Was it excitement, stress, peer pressure, boredom, or something else?

3. Circle the top two changes you could make right now to fix the slip. These might include returning something, cutting out extra spending for a couple weeks, or putting a reminder on your phone before the next payment due date.

Taking a few minutes for this kind of review flips the mindset from guilt to action and builds the kind of habits that matter way more than perfection. Recovery skills get stronger each time you use them, and pretty soon, small slip-ups feel routine to solve.

Social pressures keep showing up. Maybe your group starts talking about a concert or the newest phone, making it feel almost impossible not to join in. The next time you see your budget sliding off track, circle back to the pattern: notice what's happening, admit it without drama, then map out two clear moves to patch things up. Even if you wind up needing some support from parents or customer service, each round of recovery makes you less likely to panic in the future. By learning how to bounce back from these mistakes now, you set yourself up for a future where money problems are just temporary bumps, not disasters.

Now that you've learned how to spot common money traps like overspending, under-saving, and ignoring debt, and seen how peer pressure and FOMO can pull you off track. You have the tools to make smarter choices. Remember, everyone makes money mistakes, but what matters most is how you bounce back: by facing problems head-on, learning from them, and making a clear plan to move forward. As you practice these habits, you'll build confidence in managing your money, stand strong against outside pressure, and create a future where you're in control, not your budget or your friends' expectations. This is just the start of your journey to financial freedom, and every small step counts.

CHAPTER 10

BUILDING YOUR FINANCIAL GAME PLAN

Managing money can feel confusing or stressful, especially when you're just starting out. Many teens find themselves wondering where to begin, how to set real goals, and what habits actually help without making life more complicated. Money isn't just about numbers. It's about the choices you make every day and the freedom those choices can bring. When you understand how to take control of your finances in a way that fits your life, it stops being a mystery and starts becoming a tool for your future.

This chapter walks you through creating a financial game plan tailored just for you. You'll learn how to set clear, meaningful goals, build simple routines to track your progress, and develop a healthy respect for money that helps you stay motivated. It's not about perfection or strict rules; it's about finding practical steps that make managing your money feel doable and even enjoyable as you work toward the things that matter most to you.

Setting Your First Money Goals and How to Achieve Them

Setting your first financial goals is where your money journey truly begins. This is the moment when your plans turn into purpose. Creating clear targets makes everything else easier, such as building habits and keeping track of your progress. Think of money as a tool that helps shape your choices, not just something you are supposed to save or monitor. When you give your money a specific role, such as buying concert tickets, saving for a phone, or creating an emergency fund, you take charge of your own direction instead of following random rules.

Take a moment to imagine what life would look like if money felt simple instead of stressful. Would you be ready for new adventures with friends? Would you sleep better knowing you have something set aside for unexpected plans? Choose a goal that truly matters to you, not one that someone else expects. It does not need to be a lifelong dream. It is just a target that helps you focus your attention right now. Maybe you want to see your favorite band soon, save one thousand dollars after graduation, or build a small safety cushion so you never worry about late payments. A goal like that gives you real motivation.

Clear goals help you decide what to do with the money that comes in. They also make it easier to avoid spending on impulse because you already know what matters most to you. When temptation hits, like grabbing an extra snack or joining friends for another outing, remind yourself that every choice brings you closer to something important.

A simple way to turn a wish into a goal is to use the SMART method. SMART means Specific, Measurable, Achievable, Relevant, and Time based. Instead of saying that you want to save money, create a plan you can actually complete. For example, imagine you want to save two hundred dollars for new headphones within four months. That goal is specific and has a clear finish line. Divide two hundred by four months and you will need fifty dollars each month, which is about twelve dollars and fifty cents every week. That makes your goal measurable and realistic. If you can save that amount without giving up all your fun, it is achievable. Relevant means it is something that matters to you personally. Time based means you have a clear deadline that keeps you motivated.

Write your goal somewhere you will see it every day, such as your phone wallpaper, mirror, or notebook. Every time you look at it, it will remind you what you are working toward. A goal that stays only in your mind is easy to forget, but one that you see often stays alive. The more you track your progress, such as adding twelve dollars and fifty cents each week, the more confident you will feel. Every small step becomes proof that you are a person who sets goals and achieves them.

Big goals can feel a little intimidating at first, but breaking them into smaller pieces makes them much easier to handle. Imagine you want to save six hundred dollars for a laptop within one year. That equals fifty dollars a month. Each time you reach your monthly target, check it off and celebrate your progress with a simple reward. You could host a movie night at home with snacks, take a long walk while listening to your favorite playlist, or buy a small pack of stickers for your laptop. Try to skip the random impulse purchases that might throw your plan off course. Choose rewards that make you feel proud and motivated rather than ones that drain your savings.

Motivation can fade over time, especially when progress feels slow or distractions pop up. A few simple tricks can help you stay focused. Set reminders on your phone to save money each week. Find a friend who also has a goal and check in with each other by sending quick messages or funny memes when you both make progress. Add a calendar note every two weeks to review how far you have come. You can also make a visual tracker by drawing a bar or filling in boxes every time you save. Seeing your success build in front of you makes it more exciting to keep going.

If something unexpected happens, such as an extra expense or a tough week, remember that it does not mean you have failed. Adjust your goal, change the timeline, or make the steps smaller. The plan is yours, not a test that can go wrong.

Now let's make this real with a goal setting activity you can use right now. Grab a piece of paper or open the notes app on your phone. Think of one thing you want to achieve that feels realistic and meaningful within the next few months. Write it at the top of the page, and then answer the following questions.

1. What's the exact amount you need?
2. By what date do you want to reach this?
3. Break it into smaller chunks. (How much each month or week?)
4. Where will you keep track? (Notebook, app, wall chart)
5. How will you celebrate each mini-milestone?

Example:

- Save $300 for a weekend trip in 6 months.
- $300 ÷ 6 = $50 each month.
- Track on a phone calendar.
- Celebrate each $50 with a solo coffee run.

Your own template:

- Save $______ for ________ in _______ months.
- That's $______ each month or $______ each week.
- Track my win here: _________.
- Celebrate every _________ with __________.

Building goals and habits is like setting your personal autopilot. Each small success proves to yourself what's possible. Pretty soon, daily and weekly routines roll out, making decisions easier and the journey to your goal smoother. That's when managing your money shifts from feeling tricky to something you actually enjoy.

Creating a Simple Money Routine and Tracking Progress

Momentum begins when you take a goal, such as saving twenty five dollars from your first paycheck, and turn it into something you can repeat. What happens after that first step matters more than the one time win. When a new saver checks their progress after a week and sees that the twenty five dollars is still there, it feels real. Looking at what worked, noticing what felt difficult, and celebrating a small win all add up to lasting motivation. That feeling turns money goals from something on a wish list into something that grows steadily in real life.

Creating routines is not about being strict or following complicated rules. The goal is to make your financial life feel calmer and easier to manage. When you set a regular time to check your money, you remove the stress of thinking about it all the time. Instead of worrying at random moments, you know when to review things, and that brings peace of mind. Routines also build confidence. Even if you miss a week, the habit stays with you and is simple to restart.

Your routine can be as small or flexible as you need it to be. Choose a time each week that fits your schedule, like Sunday evening before bed, Friday afternoon after school, or during a quiet moment on the bus ride home. If you play sports or have a busy schedule, open a note on your phone and write down what you earned or spent. Add an emoji to show how you felt about it. If you have a weekend job, try using a budgeting app to check your balance every Sunday night. Take a few minutes to record what came in and what went out. If you earn cash tips, make a habit of placing the money in clearly labeled envelopes and take a quick photo each time as a reminder of your progress.

Sample Weekly Money Routine

Here's a guide to building a weekly check-in that really sticks:

1. Choose your "money check-in" time. Look for a spot where you have at least five calm minutes every week.
2. Grab your usual tool; phone, notebook, or app.
3. List all sources of money from the week. This can include jobs, allowance, odd jobs, or gifts.
4. Write down or track what you spent, no matter the amount.
5. Highlight your "win of the week". Maybe it's saying no to an expensive snack, saving spare change, or hitting a savings target.
6. Mark progress with a sticker, star, or quick snapshot on your phone.
7. Set a mini-goal for next week. Keep it realistic, like saving $5 more or tracking every purchase.
8. That's it. Close your notebook or swipe away your app. You're done until next week.

Making this routine a little playful gives it staying power. Use a progress chart on your wall, add colorful stickers, or share goals with a friend who's doing the same thing. Each week's check-in feels like a quick win rather than a chore.

Tracking Wins and Staying Engaged

Turning money tracking into something rewarding keeps it from getting boring. Celebrate even small milestones. Every time you resist an impulse buy, call it out and jot it down. Did you compare prices before spending? Snap a photo of your best find. These little victories add up and make the process feel personal.

You don't need a fancy app. Most phones have note functions, and a simple journal or piece of paper works just as well. Keeping the tools easy to use means you'll stick with it. If you ever miss a week, don't stress. The goal is to keep coming back, building stability over time.

Reviewing and Updating

Money habits work best when they grow and change along with your life. Once each month, take a few minutes to look back at your progress. Review your wins, your check ins, and the goals you set for saving or spending. Ask yourself questions such as, Did I reach my goal? Is there anything I want to adjust? Maybe your summer job allows you to save a little extra, or you realize you have been spending more than you planned on snacks. Write down what you want to do differently next month. Think of this as checking your stats in a favorite video game. It is a way to level up, not something to feel guilty about.

Updating your plan gives you freedom to respond to changes in life without worry or shame. If a system is not working, adjust it. Flexibility gives you control and keeps your money plan useful no matter what happens. You can always test a new method or create a smaller step if you feel stuck.

The more consistent you become with your money routines, the more confidence and independence you will feel. Money turns into something you guide, rather than something that guides you. In chapter ten, you will explore the idea that money creates freedom and how learning to respect it opens new opportunities in your life, even when you are just getting started. Building small, steady habits now lays the foundation for feeling capable, confident, and ready for anything that comes next.

Understanding Money as Freedom and Treating It with Respect

Routines that help you track your goals give you a clear sense of progress, but it is even more powerful when you understand why you are doing it. When you start thinking about money as more than just paper bills or numbers in an app, you realize it represents choice. It gives you the ability to decide what to do, where to go, how to spend your time, and which opportunities to take. Imagine saving enough for that concert ticket you have been dreaming about, or having a little extra for a fun night out with friends. Maybe you are planning ahead for a summer activity or feel confident knowing you could replace your phone if it breaks. That is what real independence looks like, and money is the tool that helps you create it.

Money is not only what you earn from a job or receive as a gift. It becomes something that opens doors when you treat it with care and purpose. With savings, you can choose the college that excites you, plan a trip with people you love, or join a program that helps you grow. You no longer need to wait for someone else to approve your choices or cover your expenses. Even a small balance in your account can bring peace of mind when unexpected things happen, like a bus repair, a last minute project, or a forgotten school fee. It keeps you in control instead of leaving you dependent on luck or others. True independence begins when you know you can handle life's surprises one step and one balance at a time.

How Respect Builds Confidence

Treating money with respect is not about being afraid of it or counting every penny. It means understanding the effort behind every dollar and making choices that match what truly matters to you. Begin with simple steps, such as reviewing your bank statements and noticing patterns. Did you spend more on snacks than you thought? Was there a small fee you missed? Paying attention to your money tells your brain that it deserves care. Before you spend or swipe, take a short pause and ask yourself if this is something you really want or just a habit. Could you wait a few days or find it cheaper somewhere else?

Respect also shows up in planning ahead. When you are thinking about a larger purchase, such as headphones, a bike, or tickets to a show, do a bit of research first. Write down a few places that sell what you want, compare prices, and check reviews. Looking before you buy helps you stay confident, avoid regret, and get the best value for your money. These decisions are not only financial; they reflect your ability to think clearly and stay committed to your goals even when temptations appear.

Building habits makes this process easier. Try setting a weekly time to check your balances or open your banking app for a quick review. This small ritual keeps your spending on track. Give your savings account a name that connects to your goals, such as Italy Trip Fund, Photography Gear, or First Car. Each time you move money into it, you are linking your effort to something exciting and personal.

When you treat money with care, you take control of your future instead of letting life push you around. Imagine planning your budget for the month, sticking to it, and watching your savings increase each week. Seeing progress, like watching a progress bar fill up, gives you energy to keep going. You feel capable because you are turning small choices into real results.

Of course, motivation can fade. You might feel tempted to spend when friends invite you out or when boredom strikes. The key is to pause and ask yourself what will feel better later: a quick treat now or being able to say yes to something bigger that you really want. Think about how proud you felt the last time you reached a goal or avoided running short on money.

Control comes from having choices. When you know where your money goes, you can spend on what matters, skip what does not, and still have enough left for surprises. Unexpected costs feel smaller when you are prepared. Confidence grows every time you follow a plan and stick to it. Even if you slip up sometimes, the respect you give to your money brings more freedom, fewer regrets, and a life guided by your own decisions.

Now that you know how to set clear goals, build simple routines, and track your progress, managing money will start to feel less like work and more like steering your own path. It is not about being perfect or having every answer. It is about making small, steady choices that add up to real control. As you practice, saving, spending, and planning will feel natural and even enjoyable. Keep your goals personal, celebrate your progress, and adjust as you grow. With this foundation, you are ready to take on new challenges and move closer to lasting financial freedom, one step at a time.

PASS THE MAP: SHARE WHAT YOU'VE LEARNED WITH OTHERS

One truth never changes: *what we share can change someone else's path.*

So here's something to think about. **If you had the chance to help another teen avoid the stress of being broke, confused, or stuck when it comes to money, would you take it?**

Picture this: a teen just like you picks up ***Financial Literacy for Teens Made Easy***. They're scrolling online, stressed about their allowance, first job, or even planning for college. They want answers that *actually make sense*. When they read your honest review, it could be the exact push they need to say: *"Okay, this book can really help me."*

That's why your voice matters. Please take a moment to leave an **honest review**—what you liked, what was useful, what clicked, or even what you think could be better. Your review won't just help me as the author. It will help other teens take control of their money, their choices, and their future.

Leaving a review is more than just feedback. It's like passing along a map. You've started learning how to budget, save, and invest, and your words could guide someone else who's just starting out.

Thank you for being part of this bigger mission. And if you know a friend or classmate who's ready to level up their money game, share the book with them, you never know how far your influence can go.

CONCLUSION

Wow, look at everything you have accomplished! Think back to when you first opened this book. Maybe you rolled your eyes and thought, "Money topics are boring, confusing, or only for adults." But now, things feel different. Whether you have started working a part time job, saving for your first car, or just opened your very first bank account, you are already far ahead of the game. You stayed focused, kept learning, and didn't let endless videos, memes, or confusing jargon pull you away from something powerful: gaining real confidence with your own money.

Take a moment to celebrate that. You could have ignored it all and told yourself you would figure it out later, the way most people do. But you didn't. That decision matters. You chose to learn about earning, spending, saving, and investing right now, while it can truly shape your future. A year, five years, or even a decade from today, you will look back and realize that starting early was one of the best gifts you ever gave yourself.

Here is the truth: nobody wakes up one morning magically knowing how to handle money like a professional. There is no specific age where everything suddenly makes sense. Even adults struggle with bills, credit, or saving for big goals. The difference is that you have already started asking questions while others are still waiting for answers to appear. That curiosity gives you an incredible advantage, because every bit of knowledge you gain now will grow in value over time.

It is completely normal if some things still feel uncertain. No one expects you to be a financial expert overnight. The world of money changes quickly, with new apps, new tools, and new trends coming and going. What feels essential today might seem unnecessary tomorrow. But you now have something that never fades: the mindset, the awareness, and the ability to make smart choices based on what really matters to you.

Maybe you were surprised to learn that budgeting is not about missing out but about making sure you always have what you need while still having fun. Maybe credit or investing once sounded impossible until you realized that small steps can grow into big results. Or maybe you finally understand why building good habits matters so much, and how those tiny decisions, repeated over time, can change everything.

Everything adds up. Every new word you learned, every exercise you tried, and every story you explored are more than random facts to remember. They are tools that help you build an amazing future one small step at a time. While some people keep guessing or hoping things will just work out, you are already building a solid foundation for your goals.

Here is another truth worth remembering. You do not have to do this by yourself. You may know more about money than many people your age, but that does not mean you should stop asking for help. The smartest people never stop learning or reaching out for advice. Parents, teachers, mentors, and friends can all be great resources. Ask questions, listen to their stories, and learn what worked for them and what did not. Your journey is your own, but it becomes stronger when you share it with others.

Some of your friends might ignore money topics or say it is too boring to care about. They will understand later, often after making expensive mistakes. That will not be you, because you have already made the choice to show up for yourself. It might feel strange to be the friend who keeps a budget or says, "That is not in my plan right now," when everyone else is spending without thinking. Stay confident. Trust what you have learned. In time, your calm attitude will stand out, and people will start turning to you for advice.

Take a moment to picture your future self. Imagine opening your banking app and seeing your balance grow instead of shrink. Picture having options when it is time for college, a trip, or your first apartment because you planned ahead and saved. Think about how good it will feel to say yes to the experiences that truly matter, instead of regretting quick purchases or worrying about debt. This is your life, your goals, and your decisions.

All the pages you read, the notes you wrote, and the activities you completed will only matter if you take action. That is where the real change happens. The next step does not need to be huge. Real progress begins with one small move. Choose something simple and do it. You could track your spending for a week in your notes app, talk with your parents about opening a savings account, set a reminder to save part of your next payment, or follow a few finance experts who share smart ideas. Each small step builds momentum. The most important part is to start today.

Forget perfection. The goal is progress, not getting straight A's in Adulting 101. Even one small action proves to yourself that you're not just talking - you're walking the walk. Do that, and you'll build momentum faster than you can imagine. Each good decision gives you more energy and excitement for the next one.

If you're feeling stuck deciding where to start, flip back through these pages. What jumped out at you? Where did you think, "Whoa, that would make my life easier"? Start there. Make a quick list, circle one thing, and commit to trying it this week. You don't have to overhaul your whole life in one shot. All big journeys begin with a single step, and you already took several just by reading this book.

One last thing: Be kind to yourself along the way. You'll mess up. Everyone does. Even millionaires, even the professionals who write money books. The key is to notice what happened, learn something, and move forward. No shame. No panic. Just a little more wisdom each time.

Remember, you're not waiting for permission to grow and succeed anymore. You're in control now. You chose to show up for your future, and that's something to be proud of. It's high school graduation, your first paycheck, and your first big purchase. They're all just around the corner. You know more than you think, and you're ready for whatever comes next. So, pick your action, take that leap, and start building the life you want. One smart choice at a time.

Your future self is already thanking you. You've got this.

Made in the USA
Monee, IL
04 November 2026

67381295R00075